This study of the 1870 and 1890 Ghost Dance movements among North American Indians offers an innovative theory about why these movements arose when they did. Emphasizing the demographic situation of American Indians prior to the movements, Professor Thornton argues that the Ghost Dances were deliberate efforts to accomplish a demographic revitalization of American Indians following their virtual collapse. By joining the movements, he contends, tribes sought to assure survival by increasing their numbers through returning the dead to life.

Thornton supports this thesis empirically by closely examining the historical context of the two movements and by assessing tribal participation in them, revealing particularly how population size and decline influenced participation among and within American Indian tribes. He also considers American Indian population change after the Ghost Dance periods and shows that participation in the movements actually did lead the way to a demographic recovery for certain tribes. This occurred, Thornton argues, not, of course, by returning dead American Indians to life, but by creating enhanced tribal solidarity. This solidarity enabled participating tribes to maintain their membership at a historical point when American Indians were socially and biologically "migrating" away from tribal populations.

As well as being of intrinsic interest, Thornton's findings have broad implications for the study of revitalization and other social movements. They are particularly important with regard to the circumstances fostering social movements and the rational basis of social movement participation.

Other books in the series

J. Milton Yinger, Kiyoshi Ikeda, Frank Laycock, and Stephen J. Cutler: *Middle Start: An Experiment in the Educational Enrichment of Young Adolescents*

James A. Geschwender: *Class, Race, and Worker Insurgency: The League of Revolutionary Black Workers*

Paul Ritterband: *Education, Employment, and Migration: Israel in Comparative Perspective*

John Low-Beer: *Protest and Participation: The New Working Class in Italy*

Orrin E. Klapp: *Opening and Closing: Strategies of Information Adaptation in Society*

Rita James Simon: *Continuity and Change: A Study of Two Ethnic Communities in Israel*

Marshall B. Clinard: *Cities with Little Crime: The Case of Switzerland*

Steven T. Bossert: *Tasks and Social Relationships in Classrooms: A Study of Instructional Organization and Its Consequences*

Richard E. Johnson: *Juvenile Delinquency and Its Origins: An Integrated Theoretical Approach*

David R. Heise: *Understanding Events: Affect and the Construction of Social Action*

Ida Harper Simpson: *From Student to Nurse: A Longitudinal Study of Socialization*

Stephen P. Turner: *Sociological Explanation as Translation*

Janet W. Salaff: *Working Daughters of Hong Kong: Filial Piety or Power in the Family?*

Joseph Chamie: *Religion and Fertility: Arab Christian–Muslim Differentials*

William Friedland, Amy Barton, and Robert Thomas: *Manufacturing Green Gold: Capital, Labor, and Technology in the Lettuce Industry*

Richard N. Adams: *Paradoxical Harvest: Energy and Explanation in British History, 1870–1914*

Mary F. Rogers: *Sociology, Ethnomethodology, and Experience: A Phenomenological Critique*

James R. Beniger: *Trafficking in Drug Users: Professional Exchange Networks in the Control of Deviance*

Jon Miller: *Pathways in the Workplace: The Effects of Race and Gender on Access to Organizational Resources*

Andrew J. Weigert, J. Smith Teitge, and Dennis Teitge: *Society and Identity: Toward a Sociological Psychology*

Michael A. Faia: *The Strategy and Tactics of Dynamic Functionalism*

Joyce Rothschild-Whitt and J. Allen Whitt: *The Cooperative Workplace: Potentials and Dilemmas of Organizational Democracy and Participation*

**The Arnold and Caroline Rose Monograph Series
of the American Sociological Association**

We shall live again

We shall live again

**The 1870 and 1890 Ghost Dance
movements as demographic revitalization**

Russell Thornton

University of Minnesota

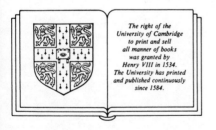

The right of the
University of Cambridge
to print and sell
all manner of books
was granted by
Henry VIII in 1534.
The University has printed
and published continuously
since 1584.

Cambridge University Press

Cambridge
London   New York   New Rochelle
Melbourne   Sydney

Published by the Press Syndicate of the University of Cambridge
The Pitt Building, Trumpington Street, Cambridge CB2 1RP
32 East 57th Street, New York, NY 10022, USA
10 Stamford Road, Oakleigh, Melbourne 3166, Australia

First published 1986

Printed in the United States of America

Library of Congress Cataloging-in-Publication Data
Thornton, Russell, 1942–
We shall live again.
(The Arnold and Caroline Rose monograph series of
the American Sociological Association)
Bibliography: p.
Includes index.
1. Ghost dance. 2. Indians of North America – West
(U.S.) – Population. 3. Indians of North America – West
(U.S.) – Rites and ceremonies. I. Title. II. Series.
E98.D2T48 1986   304.6'08997078   86–4176

British Library Cataloguing in Publication Data
Thornton, Russell
We shall live again : the 1870 and 1890 Ghost
Dance movements as demographic revitalization. –
(The Arnold and Caroline Rose monograph series
of the American Sociological Association)
1. Ghost dance   2. Demography – North America
3. Indians of North America – Population
I. Title   II. Series
299'.7   E98.D2

ISBN 0 521 32894 2

For
   all those who danced the Dances
   and
To
   Russell and Rebecca, who never did

My children, when at first I liked the whites,
My children, when at first I liked the whites,
I gave them fruits,
I gave them fruits.

  – Arapaho Ghost Dance song

Father, have pity on me,
Father, have pity on me;
I am crying for thirst,
I am crying for thirst;
All is gone – I have nothing to eat,
All is gone – I have nothing to eat.

– Arapaho Ghost Dance song

We shall live again,
We shall live again.

  – Comanche Ghost Dance song

Contents

Preface

Two social movements arose among American Indian peoples in the latter nine-teenth century – the 1870 Ghost Dance and the 1890 Ghost Dance. Each had the same objective: to restore American Indian societies devastated by contact with Europeans. The restorations were to occur through the performance of prescribed dances and were to include the removal of whites from Indian lands; reappear-ance of animal and plant food supplies, specifically the buffalo; and elimination of disease. They were also to include the return of American Indian dead to life; thus the name "Ghost" Dances.

Each Ghost Dance movement has received a variety of scholarly attention, from descriptions of the performance of actual dances, to cultural, social, even psychological explanations, to empirical research on tribal participation. My work, reported here, examines the conditions that fostered the Ghost Dance movements and tribal participation in them.

In contrast to prior scholarship on these movements, I emphasize the demo-graphic situations of American Indians. My thesis is that the Ghost Dance move-ments were meant to accomplish a *demographic revitalization*. By joining the movements, tribes might assure their survival by increasing their numbers through returning the dead to life, which was the most fundamental objective of both movements. From this point of view, the Ghost Dances were deliberate attempts to respond to a threatening situation rather than a phenomenon of mass hysteria.

I show, empirically, that the Ghost Dances were attempts at demographic revitalization. I do so by discussing the historical context in which they occurred and by assessing tribal participation in detail and examining how demographic and related considerations influenced it, both among and within American Indian tribes.

I also consider what happened to American Indian tribes after the Ghost Dance periods. For complicated reasons, each of the two movements was eventually successful for participant tribes, and each did lead the way to a demographic revival for them.

Although I limit my research to the 1870 and 1890 American Indian Ghost Dances as demographic revitalizations, it should prove pertinent to the study of other revitalization movements, Indian or non-Indian, in different ways, as well as to the consideration of social movements generally. I hope my work makes a contribution to research and debates of other scholars.

Particularly important in this regard are the circumstances fostering or hindering such movements (see, for example, Jorgensen, 1972; Champagne, 1983; Jenkins, 1983; and Olzak, 1983). My view, presented here and elsewhere (Thornton, 1981, 1982, 1984c), is that basic population changes are important antecedents to the occurrence of social movements. My additional view, also presented here and elsewhere (Thornton, 1984c), is that the demographic changes may be considered threats to the integrity of group boundaries and are met by collective efforts, particularly revitalization movements, to reaffirm dissolving boundaries.

In Chapter 1, I provide a brief, general discussion of the Ghost Dance movements for those unfamiliar with them. Chapter 2 is a consideration of previous scholarship examining the movements; there I discuss various ways the movements have been discussed and researched.

Chapter 3 sets forth my basic view of the Ghost Dances as demographic revitalization and the general hypothesis guiding my research. Chapter 4 is a discussion of the general historic context in which the movements occurred and is the initial test of my hypothesis.

In Chapter 5, I examine both inter- and intratribal differences in Ghost Dance participation, relating both to selected demographic, demographic-type, and associated variables. Chapter 6 presents an assessment of the post–Ghost Dance population recovery of the tribes in question, by relating tribal differences in participation to subsequent population changes and maintenance of full-blood tribal populations.

A final chapter offers a summary and a conclusion, along with some implications of my view of the Ghost Dances and my empirical findings.

Appendix A presents in a single form the contingency tables used in my statistical analysis; Appendix B is a detailed statement of methodological considerations underlying the data of this analysis; and Appendixes C through H contain the basic data themselves.

Acknowledgments

Portions of this work have been published previously in Thornton (1981, 1982). The present work is both an elaboration and an extension of these publications.

I have made oral presentations of various parts of the work on two occasions at the D'Arcy McNickle Center for the History of the American Indian of the Newberry Library (Chicago) and on single occasions at the Departments of Sociology of UCLA and the Florida State University, at the Population Research Laboratory of the University of Southern California, at the National Institute of Mental Health, and at the 1984 meeting of the American Society for Ethnohistory. I thank more colleagues than I am able to recall for comments at these presentations.

The encouragement of Tony Paredes in the Department of Anthropology at Florida State University was very helpful in the early stages of this research. He was kind enough to read an early draft of the entire manuscript. Ron Aminzade in the Department of Sociology at the University of Minnesota provided freely his knowledge of social movements and commented on the final chapter.

Reviewers of earlier drafts of the manuscript additionally provided very insightful and thus very helpful critiques. I am much indebted to them for their anonymous efforts. I am also much indebted to Ernest Campbell in the Department of Sociology and Anthropology at Vanderbilt University, editor of the Rose Monograph Series, for nonanonymous comments.

Gloria DeWolfe, Joanne Losinski, and Mary Ann Beneke, of the supportive staffs of the Department of Sociology and the Family Study Center of the University of Minnesota, spent hours at typewriters and word processors preparing versions of the manuscript. Gloria DeWolfe deserves particular praise in this regard. Thank you, Gloria!

I recognize the editorial skills of Martha Roth, now the managing editor of *Contemporary Sociology*, who did wonders for an early version of the manuscript.

Finally, the research was conducted under the auspices of a Research Scientist Career Development Award from the National Institute of Mental Health (No. 5-K01-MH00256). The support is much appreciated.

1. The 1870 and 1890 Ghost Dance movements

The Ghost Dances of 1870 and 1890 were similar social movements among American Indian peoples of the western United States. Both originated near the Walker River Reservation in western Nevada. The early prophets of both movements belonged to the same Paviotso (Northern Paiute) tribe (one disciple of the 1870 dance appears even to have been the father of the originator of the 1890 dance, though there is scholarly debate on this issue).[1] Both movements sought similar objectives, especially the return to life of American Indian dead (Kroeber, 1904: 34–35). And both movements included similar tribal rituals of songs and circular dances (Kroeber, 1925:868).

Despite such similarities, each movement was in fact distinct. They occurred approximately twenty years apart. They also covered basically different geographical areas, with only some slight overlap. The 1870 Ghost Dance spread from its late 1860s origin in extreme western Nevada throughout most of Nevada and into Oregon and California, where it was probably strongest and certainly most pervasive. The 1890 Ghost Dance began from virtually the same Nevada location in the late 1880s and reached throughout the state, but only slightly westward into Oregon and California; it spread primarily to the north, east, and south, affecting Indian peoples in Idaho, Montana, Utah, the Dakotas, Oklahoma Territory, New Mexico, Arizona, and other states as well. Eventually it encompassed most of the central western United States, in contrast to the far more limited area of the 1870 Ghost Dance. (See Map 1.1.)

For these reasons, the two movements are properly treated separately.

The 1870 Ghost Dance movement

The originator of the 1870 Ghost Dance was a Paviotso man named Wodziwob. The movement began when Wodziwob fell into a trance and brought from it the idea that the spirits of Indian dead could return and change the earth into a

---

[1] Mooney (1896:701) mistakenly attributed the origin of the 1870 movement to Tavivo or Numataivo, a disciple of Wodziwob and the father of Wovoka, the originator of the 1890 movement. This issue produced some scholarly confusion (see, for example, Kroeber, 1925:868), until it was apparently clarified by Du Bois (1939:3–4). Wovoka would have been in his mid-teens at the time of the 1870 movement (Mooney, 1896:764).

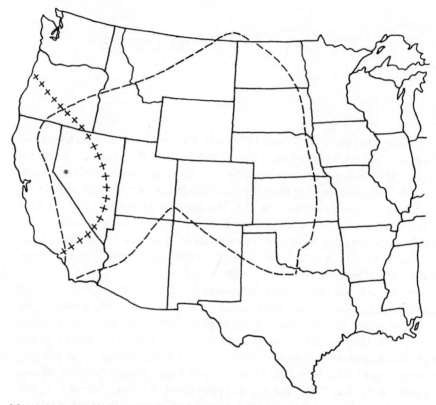

Map 1.1. Areas of the 1870 (+) and 1890 (−) Ghost Dance movements and approximate place of origin (*)

paradise for Indians. Eternal life for all Indians and the disappearance of all whites were associated features of Wodziwob's vision (Mooney, 1896:702; Du Bois, 1939:4). Wodziwob's trance took place some time in the late 1860s, and the probable date of his first actual teaching is 1869 (Du Bois, 1939:4).

Disciples spread his revelation to other Indian groups. The primary disciple seems to have been Weneyuga (Frank Spencer), a prophet of the movement in his own right, but other disciples were also involved, including one named Tavivo or Numataivo (Du Bois, 1939:6). According to some scholars, Wodziwob lived until about 1918 and was arrested for practicing shamanism a few years before he died on the Walker River Reservation (Hittman, 1973:267).

Objectives

As the 1870 movement grew, elements were added to Wodziwob's original prophecies. What additions were made depended in part on which American

Indian tribe received the teachings from which disciple at which point in time.[2] The additions also depended on the nature of the tribe in question, with each tribe adapting the prophecies to its own context and culture.

A further common theme was the return of animals, fish, and other food in abundance (see Mooney, 1896:703; Spier, 1927:47; and Du Bois, 1939:10). Another involved change in the relations between Indians and whites, not necessarily the elimination of all whites. Thus some said that "the whites were to burn up and disappear without even leaving ashes" (Du Bois, 1939:10); but others said that there would be no distinctions between the races; and still others said that the races would be eternally separate (Mooney, 1896:703).

Despite these and other somewhat divergent themes, according to Kroeber (1904:34), the single overriding idea of the 1870 Ghost Dance movement was "the belief in the return of the dead." This quickly became the central focus and apparently persisted as such throughout the movement (Du Bois, 1939:5–12). It took several specific forms, however: Sometimes the "Supreme Ruler" was to bring spirits of the dead back to earth (Mooney, 1896:703); sometimes dead relatives would be returning from the south (Du Bois, 1939:7); sometimes "the dead would come from the east when the grass was about 8 inches high" (Du Bois, 1939:10); sometimes the dead would return in armies from the rising sun (Du Bois, 1939:15); and sometimes the dead would return from their graves (Du Bois, 1939:22). In at least one instance, the return of the dead was linked directly with the destruction of whites: Kroeber (1904:34), citing Powers (1877), asserts that northern California Indians believed that their "dead would return . . . and would sweep the whites from the earth."

Ceremony

The movement held that these prophesied events would be realized if American Indian peoples performed an actual "ghost dance." The dance was probably originally an existing Paviotso round dance, employed for all special occasions. In it, men and women joined hands in a circle, then rotated the circle to the left, with a shuffling side step. Unlike many American Indian dances, it was not restricted to a special site but could be performed almost anywhere. Facial painting was involved in the ceremony as well, but it also was apparently only the usual Paviotso type. Because originally the 1870 Ghost Dance had no unique ceremony, its distinguishing features among the Paviotso were the visions experienced by the disciples and prophets during the dances and the resulting songs of participants (Du Bois, 1939:6–7).

From the original Paviotso round dance, the 1870 ceremony underwent mod-

---

[2] There were also occasional arguments about the prophecies between the disciples and Wodziwob and consequent changes in them (Du Bois, 1939:130).

ifications as performed by different tribes, just as the movement's objectives and the way they would occur changed as well. The dance was performed in a large circle by some Indians at some times; by others at other times it was danced in two or even ten circles, revolving alternately in opposite directions. The dance was performed indoors by some tribes, out-of-doors by others; in the morning by some, at night by some (Kroeber, 1904:33); sometimes around a pole, sometimes without one. It was performed in some instances with men and women separated and in others with the sexes mixed. Some tribes performed virtually naked and others fully dressed; some performed after ceremonial bathing, others did not; some waved handkerchiefs during the dance; some used a "claprattle" (Spier, 1927:47–51); and some used special colors and designs of paint, one for men and one for women (Gayton, 1930:67).

Despite these changes, two central elements from the original Paviotso round dance stayed with the ceremony throughout the duration of this first Ghost Dance movement: the circular motion from left to right and the clasping of hands by the participants. Other Paviotso characteristics also often remained. As Du Bois (1939:7) explains:

Foreign tribes in accepting the prophecies, not only placed them in a new context, but also attached to them Paviotso traits which were merely in solution among the originators. In the process of doctrinal borrowing they made these common Paviotso traits necessary concomitants of the cult. In fact, they may almost be said to have created the cult as a dynamic and specific movement.

Area

The 1870 movement spread quickly in western Nevada to adjacent bands of Paviotso and Paiute, then into the nearer parts of California and Oregon. The dance was taken up early by the Washo of Nevada and California, the Klamath of Oregon, and the Modoc of Oregon and California (Spier, 1927; Du Bois, 1939:129; Nash, 1955 [1937]). It apparently did not spread far beyond this immediate area until after 1870; but from 1871 on, it did spread quickly in all four directions, eventually through much of Oregon and California, where it was performed by tribes extending south through the San Joaquin Valley (Kroeber, 1925:868–72; Gayton, 1930; Du Bois, 1939:129). Knowledge of the movement apparently even reached the so-called mission tribes along the southern California coast (Kroeber, 1925:870–72).

Indian peoples eventually participating in the dance and its later manifestations were the Achumawi; Alsea; Atsugwei; Bannock; Cahto; Calapuya; Chilula; Coos; Costanoan; Gosiute; Huchnom; Karok; Klamath; Konkow; Lassiki; the Coast, Eastern, and Lake Miwok; Modoc; Monache; Nisenan; Nomlaki; Paiute; Patwin; Paviotso; Pomo; Santiam; Shasta; Shoshone; Siuslaw; Tolowa; Tututni; Umpqua;

Ute; Wailaki; Wappo; Washo; Whilkut; Wintu; Yana; Yokuts; Yoncalla; Yuki; and Yurok. (The Ghost Dance is even said to have spread to the Mormons, though this claim may not be true. See Mooney, 1896:703–04.)

As the movement spread among American Indian peoples, it developed three distinct manifestations: the Earth Lodge Cult, the *Bole-Maru,* and the Big Head Cult, an offshoot of the *Bole-Maru.*

The Earth Lodge Cult originated among the Northern Yana shortly after 1870 and spread to the Hill Patwin, Lake and Coast Miwok, Cahto, Wintu, Shasta, Achumawi, Wappo, Coast Yuki, Sinkyone, Pomo, and Nomlaki, as well as to several Indian peoples in Oregon (Bean and Vane, 1978:670). Its tenets were that the destruction of the world was imminent and that survival depended upon performing proper rituals in earth lodges.

Some have asserted that the Earth Lodge Cult stressed the destruction of the world and minimized the return of the dead. Du Bois (1939:132), however, concluded differently, arguing that the idea of the return of the dead was always present and that the only reason for distinguishing between the Ghost Dance and the Earth Lodge Cult was the use of the earth lodge structure itself.

The name *Bole-Maru* comes from the combination of the Patwin and Pomo words for the cult. It developed among the Hill Patwin from the original Ghost Dance (Du Bois 1939:1) and emphasized the role of a "dreamer," that is, a person who could see into the future, and individual salvation through a supreme being. The *Bole-Maru* was particularly popular among the Pomo and Maidu, in addition to its Patwin originators (Bean and Vane, 1978:670–71).

The Big Head Cult, in turn, was a variation of the early *Bole-Maru* and was concentrated in northern California and Oregon (Du Bois, 1939:2, 117–27, 129). Both it and the *Bole-Maru* were also related by Du Bois (1939:137–38) to the idea of the resurrection of the dead, though both likely minimized that idea in favor of other objectives.

Although the 1870 Ghost Dance per se had songs, none of these have survived. Some have survived from a local Wintu "dream dance" cult of the wider *Bole-Maru* and Big Head Cults. Du Bois (1939:57) presented two of them:

> Above we shall go,
> Along the Milky Way we shall go.
> Above we shall go,
> Along the flower path we shall go.
>
> Down west, down west,
> Is where we ghosts dance.
> Down west, down west,
> Is where weeping ghosts dance,
> Is where we ghosts dance.

End of the movement

By the midpoint of the decade, the 1870 Ghost Dance movement and these three variations on it had diminished. It could be said to have ended as a social movement at that time, though the Big Head Cult was prevalent through the 1880s (Du Bois, 1939:127) and the *Bole-Maru* religion continues today (Bean and Vane, 1978:671–72). Individual tribes apparently forsook the movement either because they were forced to do so by fearful whites and government agents (see Spier, 1927:51) or because they simply lost interest, perhaps because "it didn't work" (see Gayton, 1930:81; Hittman, 1973:268–69).

The 1890 Ghost Dance movement

The second Ghost Dance movement originated with a vision by a Paviotso named Wovoka, "The Cutter." He was also known as Jack Wilson and was the son of Tavivo, the disciple of Wodziwob, originator of the 1870 movement. Wovoka's vision occurred in either 1886 or 1887, depending on how one reads Mooney (see Mooney, 1896:771–72). Whatever the date, during one of these two years Wovoka experienced a revelation at Mason Valley, Nevada, near the Walker River Reservation, directing him to

tell his people they must be good and love one another, have no quarreling, and live in peace with the whites; that they must work, and not lie or steal; that they must put away all old practices that savored of war; that if they faithfully obeyed his instructions they would at last be reunited with their friends in this other world, where there would be no more death or sickness or old age. He was then given the dance which he was commanded to bring back to his people. By performing this dance at intervals, for five consecutive days each time, they would secure this happiness to themselves and hasten the event. [Mooney, 1896:772]

The 1890 Ghost Dance movement began with the dissemination of this revelation, though it may also be traced to the 1870 movement because of the family connection. Unlike the originator of the earlier movement, however, Wovoka took an active role in spreading his Ghost Dance and relied less on disciples, though they were important to its growth.

Wovoka lived until September 20, 1932 (Stewart, 1977:219), with some continued veneration. Despite Mooney's statement (1896:927) that by 1896 Wovoka had retired to obscurity, a report from the Nevada Agency in May 1917 states that Wovoka continued to be visited occasionally by delegations from distant tribes (Stewart, 1977:221).

Objectives

As was true for the 1870 Ghost Dance, variations developed in prophecies of the new movement as it spread from tribe to tribe over the years. In some instances Indians and whites were to be one people; in others, all whites were to die; and in still others, the whites were to be driven back across the ocean to their former countries (Mooney, 1896:784–86).

Even when a prophecy was constant, the way it might occur could vary, as was the case with the 1870 movement. Given the single theme of destruction of the whites, for example, different tribal groupings thought it would happen differently. Some in the southern part of its area said that destruction would come from a cyclone; others in the west said that it would result from an earthquake; and still others in the north said that it would be attributable to a landslide (Fletcher, 1891:57).

Additional themes of the 1890 movement were also close to those of 1870, for example, restoration of game and creation of a paradise on earth (Overholt, 1974:42). Here, again, the specific form might vary widely from region to region or tribe to tribe or perhaps even within a tribe, from one subarea or subgroup to another, or from one time to another (Hill, 1944:523; Dobyns and Euler, 1967:6).

Nonetheless, the basic objective of the 1890 movement remained constant, just as it had in 1870. Central to both Ghost Dance movements was the return to life of deceased populations of American Indians: "The great underlying principle of the Ghost Dance doctrine is that the time will come when the whole Indian race, living and dead, will be reunited upon a regenerated earth, to live a life of aboriginal happiness, forever free from death, disease and misery" (Mooney, 1896:777).

Even the name of the dance projects the return of the dead to life. Some tribes called the dance by names referring to its actual performance: To the Paiute it was the "dance in a circle"; to the Shoshone, "everybody dragging"; to the Kiowa, "dance with clasped hands"; to the Comanche, "with joined hands" (Mooney, 1896:791). It was named most frequently, however, by Indians as well as by whites, for its central objective: "By the Sioux, Arapaho, and most other prairie tribes it is called the "spirit" or "ghost" dance (Sioux, *Wana'ghi' wa'chipi;* Arapaho, *Thigû'nawat*), from the fact that everything connected with it relates to the coming of the spirits of the dead from the spirit world, and by this name it has become known among the whites" (Mooney, 1896:791).

Ceremony

Actual performances of 1890 Ghost Dance ceremonies varied, as did the 1870 ceremonies. Some tribes would dance at prescribed times for several days, others only once. Some would dance around a pole, which might or might not be decorated, others around a tree, which might or might not be decorated, and others with neither tree nor pole. Some tribes included fasting and sweat baths (Mooney, 1896:chap. 11), whereas others did not. Some tribes on some occasions would "consecrate" the ground before dancing (Mooney, 1896:918), but others would not.

The dance of the Northern Cheyenne, for example, had features that were said not to be found to the south, such as four fires built at each cardinal point outside the dance circle (Grinnell, 1891:66). Sioux tribes wore the "ghost shirt," a somewhat distinguishing feature of their dance; although the Arapaho and other tribes used such shirts as well, many other tribes did not wear them. Sioux participants would not wear metal; participants from the southern tribes would wear silver (Mooney, 1896:915). The Cheyenne and Southern Arapaho had a preliminary dance, the "crow dance," that other tribes did not use (Mooney, 1896:921–22). It was performed as a "warm-up" to the Ghost Dance ceremony.

Actual performance of the dance might differ even from year to year. Dobyns and Euler (1967:6) described reported changes in the 1890 Ghost Dance ceremony among the Walapai and Havasupai: A dance in 1889 lasted all night, but one in 1891 only until midnight.

One factor that remained constant for the actual 1890 ceremony, as it had for the 1870 one, was the circle: The Ghost Dance was always a circle dance.

Also central to performances of the 1890 dances were hypnotic trances and songs, both of which linked the themes or objectives of the ceremony with the physical activity of dancing. In many performances, dancers were hypnotized by leaders or by individuals who had experienced a trance (Mooney, 1896:924). It was during trances or immediately thereafter that visions would be experienced (Grinnell, 1891:68; Mooney, 1896:923) and expressed in songs.

Mooney (1896:953–1102) reported many songs of 1890, mostly from such prairie tribes as the Arapaho, Cheyenne, Sioux, Kiowa, and Caddo, but also from the Paiute. These are somewhat problematic for analysis. They tend to be highly individualized, and a single dance might easily produce dozens of them. Some songs with special qualities, however, became part of a tribe's ceremonies and were sung as opening or closing songs. Of the two, closing songs were said to be more important and more permanent (Mooney, 1896:953). After an apparent analysis of these, Overholt (1974:56) asserts, "The two most frequent themes in the songs are the return of the dead and the restoration of the game, both of which are central to Wovoka's original teaching."

Mooney describes this Arapaho song as a call for the return of game (1896:967):

> How bright is the moonlight.
> How bright is the moonlight.
> Tonight as I ride with my load of buffalo beef.
> Tonight as I ride with my load of buffalo beef.

Songs calling for the return of the Indian dead to life are this Arapaho one (Mooney, 1896:972):

> My father did not recognize me (at first),
> My father did not recognize me (at first).
> When again he saw me,

> When again he saw me,
> He said, "You are the offspring of a crow,"
> He said, "You are the offspring of a crow."

and this Sioux one (Mooney, 1896:1070):

> Mother, come home; mother, come home.
> My little brother goes about always crying.
> My little brother goes about always crying.
> Mother, come home; mother, come home.

Both themes appear in this Sioux song (Mooney, 1896:1072):

> The whole world is coming,
> A nation is coming, a nation is coming.
> The Eagle has brought the message to the tribe.
> The father says so, the father says so.
> Over the whole earth they are coming.
> The buffalo are coming, the buffalo are coming.
> The Crow has brought the message to the tribe.
> The father says so, the father says so.

Area

From a geographic origin virtually identical with that of the 1870 movement, the 1890 Ghost Dance spread also among the Paviotso and other Paiute of Nevada and into Oregon and California, overlapping the 1870 area to some extent. In addition to the Paviotso and other Paiute, the Washo and Pit River and Tule River Indians of this area also performed it.[3] It was not pervasive there, however, particularly not in California.

Concomitantly, and in contrast to the 1870 Ghost Dance, the 1890 movement spread widely to the east, northeast, and southeast. It was performed in Idaho, Montana, Utah, Wyoming, Colorado, and the Dakotas by the Arapaho, Arikara, Assiniboin, Bannock, Cheyenne, Gosiute, Gros Ventres, Hidatsa, Mandan, Shoshone, Sioux, and Ute of these areas and even reached the Dakota Sioux in Canada (Kehoe, 1968). It also reached Nebraska, Kansas, and Oklahoma Territory, affecting the Southern Arapaho, Caddo, Comanche, Delaware, Iowa, Kansas, Kickapoo, Kiowa, Kiowa-Apache, Oto-Missouri, Pawnee, and Wichita. It was even in the Southwest and California among the Chemeheuvi, Havasupai, Kichai, Taos Pueblo, and Walapai (Mooney, 1896:pl. LXXXV).[4]

---

[3] The Pit River Indians are more or less the same as the Achumawi; the Tule River Indians are apparently those of Tule River Reservation, primarily the Yokuts but perhaps also the Kern River Indians (Tubatulabal).

[4] It is extremely difficult to ascertain the exact area of the 1890 Ghost Dance (or, for that matter, of the 1870 movement). Mooney indicated that almost all of the tribes west of the Missouri River had at least heard of it.

End of the movement

As was true for the 1870 movement, the 1890 Ghost Dance lasted but a few short years. By the mid-1890s, many tribes had ceased to perform the ceremony, surely for reasons similar to those ending the 1870 movement. Also, however, the death of Sitting Bull, a Ghost Dance leader, the massacre at Wounded Knee Creek, and related armed battles between the Sioux and U.S. government troops surely dissuaded some tribes from involvement in the 1890 Ghost Dance. Nonetheless, some tribes, especially those in Oklahoma Territory, incorporated the ceremony into tribal life for many years (Mooney, 1896:927). It has even been performed in contemporary times.

2. Prior scholarship on the Ghost Dance movements

The two Ghost Dance movements have been much studied from different scholarly perspectives. My view of the Ghost Dances as attempts at demographic revitalization is rooted partly in the existing scholarly literature on the movements. For my purposes, this literature may be adequately subsumed under four general topics: descriptive accounts, studies attributing the dances to evolutionary or unique origins, accounts of conditions of differential participation, and the study of social movements. All seem of at least some relevance to the work here presented.

Descriptions

Basic descriptions of the 1870 Ghost Dance are limited, in comparison to the 1890 dance, probably because of the time difference between the two and the larger area of the 1890 movement. The 1890 dance also occurred perhaps in closer proximity to larger populations of whites, who became aware of it either directly through observation or indirectly through word-of-mouth or newspaper accounts. Further reasons undoubtedly include the development of anthropology and ethnology as scholarly disciplines and the founding of the Bureau of American Ethnology, both during the late 1800s. Contemporary accounts of the 1890 Ghost Dance were published in scholarly sources, but no contemporary scholarly accounts of the 1870 dance are to be found.

The earliest located publication on the 1870 Ghost Dance movement is Kroeber's 1904 paper "A Ghost-dance in California," published thirty-five years after the movement's origin and fourteen years after the first publication on the 1890 movement. It is only a brief account of the dance as it was performed in California. More than twenty years later, Spier published a description of the 1870 Ghost Dance among the Klamath in Oregon (1927), and then came Gayton's important discussion of the movement in south-central California (1930).

The most important overall description of the 1870 dance, and surely the most detailed, was not published until seventy years after the movement originated. This is Du Bois's *The 1870 Ghost Dance* (1939), in which the author provides accounts of the dance in western Nevada, southern Oregon, and northern and central California but does not consider its southern extension in California. In contrast, descriptions of the 1890 Ghost Dance appeared contemporaneously, including papers by Bourke (1890), Maus (1890), Moorehead (1890, 1891), Remington (1890, 1891), Fletcher (1891), Grinnell (1891) and Phister (1891). The most important description of the movement was published only a few years later, at a time when the dance was still practiced among some tribes. This is James Mooney's classic, *The Ghost-Dance Religion and the Sioux Outbreak of 1890* (1896). For more than three years, as an emissary of the U.S. government, Mooney visited tribes involved in the movement, and he prepared an extensive report based on his observations. His report focuses on the dance among the Sioux, but it also contains detailed descriptions of various other tribes.

Considerably more recently, Dobyns and Euler (1967) described the movement among both the Walapai and the Havasupai in Arizona. Eastman (1945) provided a limited account of the dance among the Sioux and its relationship to the genocide at Wounded Knee, and Kehoe (1968) reported on the dance among a group of Sioux in Canada in the early 1900s, emphasizing its religious nature. Other descriptions may be found in Lesser (1933) and La Barre (1970). Books and papers have also been written about Wovoka, founder of the Ghost Dance of 1890 (Bailey, 1957; Stewart, 1977).

Origins: evolutionary or unique?

Whether the Ghost Dance movements represent the evolution and/or diffusion of other, similar movements has been a point of considerable debate. Spier (1935) and Suttles (1957) argued that the 1890 Ghost Dance derived from the 1870 Ghost Dance, which in turn was an evolutionary development of the Prophet Dance of the Northwest Coast. Aberle (1959) argued against this interpretation, and Mooney (1896) viewed the 1890 dance as a unique occurrence, with historical parallels but not antecedents. Herzog (1935) argued that the Ghost Dance music of the Plains tribes did not originate there but spread from the Great Basin region, and Thurman (1984) argued that there was a continuous development from the 1760 Delaware Prophet through the 1890 Ghost Dance. Spier (1935) believed that later dances and cults developed from the 1870 Ghost Dance, as did Du Bois (1939), and Du Bois paid detailed attention to the development of the Ghost Dance into the Earth Lodge Cult and the *Bole-Maru*. Meader (1967) related an 1881 social movement among the White Mountain Apache to the 1870 Ghost Dance.

Most writers, however, have seen the movements as responses to the social and cultural deprivations American Indian peoples experienced following contact with European populations. Kroeber (1925) gave various reasons why the two Ghost Dance movements spread in different directions but emphasized "cultural decay" as the general explanation. The first movement occurred among the Indians of California around 1870 and the second among the Indians of the Plains around 1890, he argued, because "the native civilization of northern California appears to have suffered as great a disintegration by 1870, 20 or 25 years after its first serious contact with whites, as the average tribe of the central United States had undergone by 1890, or from 50 to 100 years after similar contact began" (869).

Bean and Vane (1978:671–72) also explained this difference in these terms, and Lesser (1933:109) offered virtually the same explanation, although he referred only to the movement of 1890: "The Ghost Dance spread among American Indian tribes at a time when the final destruction of native cultures was well advanced."

In "Acculturation and Messianic Movements," Barber (1941) described both dances as movements in response to "harsh times" or "deprivation." Hittman (1973) analyzed conditions at the Walker River Reservation that gave rise to the 1870 Ghost Dance, including land loss, epidemics of illness, and starvation. Deprivation as the basis of the dances is discussed by Nash (1955 [1937]) and Aberle (1959) regarding the 1870 dance and by Dobyns and Euler (1967) regarding the 1890 dance.

The 1890 movement has been described as a psychological prophet or messiah process. Early mention of this theory may be found in Fletcher (1891) and Phister (1891); however, the only detailed examination seems to be Overholt's "The Ghost Dance of 1890 and the Nature of the Prophetic Process" (1974). Recently, DeMallie (1982) has discussed the 1890 Ghost Dance among the Sioux as a religious movement permeating their culture. So far as I know, no one has considered the earlier movement in this context.

According to Du Bois (1939:135–39), news of the 1870 Ghost Dance was spread deliberately, both by "missionaries" from practicing tribes and by delegates from interested tribes sent to inquire about the movement. Also according to Du Bois (135–36), local conditions that brought diverse groups of Indians together helped to spread the movement: intermarriage between tribes, the few reservations, such transportation advances as the use of the horse and the train, and the exploitation of Indian labor for agriculture in California.

The 1890 dance seems to have spread in similar ways, although the written word was probably more important. Introduction of the boarding-school system for young Indians apparently created a literate cadre for spreading word of the movement (Mooney, 1896:820) by newspapers and magazines (Remington, 1890:947) and by letters (Utley, 1963:67).

Differential acceptance

Differential acceptance of the Ghost Dances by different tribes has also been of interest to scholars. Du Bois (1939:136–37) offered explanations for both acceptance and rejection of the 1870 dance. Tribes participated because of the aesthetic appeal of the songs and dances, the emotional appeal to those bereaved by loss of family or friends, and belief in the possibilities of cultural restoration and improved economic conditions. Others rejected the dance because of insufficient deterioration of their culture, too great an acculturation to non-Indian ways, and conflict with specific doctrines, such as equating mixed-bloods with whites, or a fear of the dead.

Nash (1955 [1937]) examined the differential participation in the 1870 Ghost Dance of the Modoc, Klamath, and Paviotso (Snake?) tribes on the Klamath Reservation in Oregon. He found that while all three groups took part, the actual degree of participation varied with the extent of cultural deprivation experienced by the tribe.

Differential participation in the 1890 movement has been explained in similar ways. Both Barber (1941) and Hill (1944) discussed the lack of participation of the Navajo tribe in the 1890 Ghost Dance movement. Barber argued that whereas the Navajo had suffered deprivations during the 1860s, by the late 1880s they had returned to their lands from exile in Bosque Redondo and had reestablished themselves. By the late 1880s, their culture was restored to the extent that "when Paiute runners tried to spread the belief in the coming of the Ghost Dance Messiah, their mission was fruitless. . . . There was no social need for a redeemer" (Barber, 1941:666).

Hill (1944:525) explained the noninvolvement of the Navajo on the basis of their *fear* that the dead might return to life: "For the Navaho with his almost psychotic fear of death, the dead and all connected with them, no greater cataclysm than the return of the departed or ghosts could be envisaged. In short, the Navaho were frightened out of their wits for fear the tenets of the movement were true."

Similarly, variations in participation within a tribe have been discussed. Nash (1955 [1937]) found that intratribal differences on the Klamath Reservation were influenced by the amount of deprivation experienced, just as intertribal ones were. Dobyns and Euler (1967:28–29) discussed differential participation of Havasupai bands in 1890, but they found that the deprivation hypothesis did not explain observed differences.

Despite this history of scholarship, it was not until the 1970s that systematic research on differential participation appeared, and then only regarding the 1890 movement. Carroll (1975) sought to explain why some American Indian peoples accepted this Ghost Dance while others did not, given that all were aware of the movement. His research incorporated such variables as tribal distance from the dance's origin; social, cultural, and economic deprivations resulting from the then-recent destruction of buffalo herds; and differences in political, kinship, and inheritance structures of different tribes. He concluded that participation was not influenced by a tribe's distance from the source of the movement, that is, by cultural diffusion. The destruction of buffalo and the social structures of tribes, he found, influenced acceptance. (See, also, Champagne, 1983, for an examination of the relationship between internal tribal structure and the "institutionalization" of revitalization movements.)

Following Carroll's work, Brown (1976) correlated differential acceptance with tribal dependence on hunting and how it was affected by the destruction of buffalo herds. Landsman (1979) correlated differential acceptance with the dates of allotment of American Indian reservation land and found that tribes participating were typically those without land at the time. Carroll (1976, 1979) replied to both Brown's and Landsman's work, defending his arguments against their criticisms.

Study of social movements

The Ghost Dances have often been linked to the general study of social movements, with an emphasis on cultural loss or destruction.

Important in this regard was Linton's (1943:230) formulation of "nativistic" movements: "any conscious, organized attempt on the part of a society's members to revive or perpetuate selected aspects of its culture." Since they emphasized regaining the past, he viewed the Ghost Dances merely as two examples of nativistic movements.

More important, however, was Wallace's (1956) analysis, which included nativistic movements and named them, along with "revivalistic," "vitalistic," "utopian," and "messianic" ones, as well as "cargo cults," "revitalization movements." The general objective of these revitalization movements is, as Wallace puts it, "a deliberate, organized, conscious effort by members of a society to construct a more satisfying culture" (265). The Ghost Dances may certainly be considered as efforts to "revitalize" American Indian societies and cultures by reviving former ways of life.[1]

[1] Jorgensen (1972), following the work of David F. Aberle, discusses transformative and redemptive social movements: Transformative movements "consist of organized groups of people who actively seek a transformation of the social, even natural, order in their own lifetimes" (6); redemptive movements, in contrast, "seek total change to the individual. It is the person, not the social order, therefore, that is transformed" (7). According to Jorgensen, the Ghost Dances are examples of transformative movements.

Following Wallace's analysis, Meader (1967) and Carroll (1975) cast their respective studies of the 1870 and 1890 dances in his terms. I used them as well in my earlier examinations of both movements (Thornton, 1981, 1982).

Similarly, Lanternari (1963) discussed both dances as instances of religious movements in response to colonialism and the subsequent inability of native peoples to repel the intruders. Such movements have occurred, according to Lanternari, at various times in Asia and Indonesia, Polynesia, Melanesia, Central and South America, and Africa, as well as in North America. Finally, Worsley (1957) discussed the dances as general social movements, emphasizing their integrative functions and noting also that such movements have occurred all over the globe.

Implications

This wide variety of scholarship forms a solid basis for the work reported here. My work tries to extend this scholarship, in that my focus is on conditions fostering the occurrence of the Ghost Dances and on determinants of differential tribal participation. However, I also depart significantly from earlier scholarship: I choose to emphasize demographic explanations; I focus on the central theme of the movements, the return of the dead; and I consider the post–Ghost Dance periods in addition to times during and before the movements. All three have been neglected issues, until now.

3. Hypothesis of demographic revitalization

The hypothesis guiding my analysis of the movements may now be developed.

Background to hypothesis

My hypothesis is derived from two basic sources: (1) studies of depopulation and social movements and (2) the objective of the Ghost Dances themselves.

Depopulation

Several scholars have linked the Ghost Dance movements with the depopulation of American Indians. Brown (1976:742) noted that population loss probably explained differential acceptance of the 1890 dance but did not pursue the conclusion. Mooney (1896:826) described conditions among the Sioux prior to their involvement in the 1890 Ghost Dance, specifically, "epidemics of measles, grippe, and whooping cough, in rapid succession and with terribly fatal results," immediately before the Sioux joined in the Ghost Dance movement. Barber (1941:664, 666) also mentioned population losses as an important antecedent to the acceptance of the Ghost Dance by the Sioux in 1890.

Nash (1955 [1937]:418) and Dobyns and Euler (1967:38), respectively, asserted the connection of population decline to acceptance of the 1870 dance by tribes on the Klamath Reservation and of the 1890 Ghost Dance by the Pai. In discussing the 1870 movement among the Paiute of the Walker River Reservation in Nevada, Hittman (1973:260) stated, "Two years of epidemics which led to the death of approximately one-tenth of the Walker River Reservation Paiute population doubtless caused great stress, if not actual crises. . . . In this context, then, [the prophet] Wodziwob prophesied the resurrection of the dead, and the Walker River Reservation Paiute responded enthusiastically."

However, depopulation has typically been considered less important to the Ghost Dance movements than either social or cultural deprivation. Sometimes it has been regarded as merely another aspect of deprivation. Thus Dobyns and Euler assert that while population decline preceded Pai (Havasupai and Walapai) participation, other reasons were more important; and both Barber and Nash discuss population decline as only an aspect of cultural deprivation. My 1981

17

and 1982 publications were the first to show the importance of demographic changes alone in participation of tribes in both Ghost Dance movements, and as a cause of social and cultural deprivations associated with them.

That recent work on the movements is the first in which they have been studied demographically seems to me ironic. North American Indian social movements other than the Ghost Dances have been linked closely with depopulation following European contact. Strong (1945) related archaeological evidence of a "ghost cult" on the Columbia River to depopulation of the area, and Ford and Wiley (1941:358) made the same linkage for southern American Indian populations.

The most comprehensive statement of such a relationship is Walker's (1969) examination of the Prophet Dance controversy. Addressing Spier's (1927, 1935) hypothesis that the Prophet Dance was the source of various cults, including the Ghost Dances, and that it was itself entirely an aboriginal development predating European contact, rather than a response to cultural deprivation, Walker provided examples of the relationship between nativistic cults and depopulation (247–52).

Depopulation has also been linked to social movements similar to the Ghost Dances in other parts of the world. Lanternari (1963:224) found such links in the history of the native peoples of Australia, and Worsley (1957:146–94) found them in the Solomon Islands and the New Hebrides. Worsley discussed the rise of the Naked Cult on the island of Espiritu Santo in response to decimation of the native population. The prophet of the movement, Runovoro, had promised that "the dead would arise, and the ancestors would return from a far land where the Whites had sent them" (148).

Cohn (1970) linked medieval European millenarian movements to population changes, including those after plagues. Cohn emphasized population increase, but he argued (282) that revolutionary movements of the Middle Ages occurred in response to disasters, particularly demographic ones.

Objective

The most basic Ghost Dance objective was the return to life of dead populations of American Indians. This theme was present in the other American Indian social movements that have been linked to depopulation (Spier, 1935; Ford and Wiley, 1941; Strong, 1945; Walker, 1969) and also in the non-American Indian movements described by Worsley (1957) and Lanternari (1963). Scholars of the Ghost Dances, however, have paid more attention to the relationship between the dances and the restoration of animal popultions, particularly buffalo in the 1890 Ghost Dance (Kroeber, 1925:869; Lesser, 1933:109; Barber, 1941:664).

Hypothesis of demographic revitalization

A possible relationship between depopulation and the Ghost Dance (and other similar movements) thus suggests a hypothesis, which is that American Indian peoples sought to increase their numbers through regaining populations of the dead by performing "ghost" dances. The movements may therefore be considered deliberate efforts at demographic revitalization.

It is this hypothesis which guides the analysis of the Ghost Dance movements in subsequent chapters. The analysis is twofold: (1) I examine the historic demographic context within which the movements occurred; and (2) I conduct a quantitative study of both inter- and intratribal differences in Ghost Dance participation as associated with demographic and related variables. I also investigate the subsequent demographic effects of the movements.

4. Depopulation and the Ghost Dance movements

My hypothesis of demographic revitalization suggests that the occurrence of the Ghost Dances was linked closely to American Indian depopulation. It follows that if the movements were efforts toward such revitalization, then they would seemingly have occurred close to the time of greatest American Indian population depletion. To investigate this possibility, I here examine the historical demographic context of American Indians in the United States, particularly those living in the geographical areas of the Ghost Dances at the approximate time they occurred.

Pre-European American Indian population

Twentieth-century scholarly estimates of the aboriginal (i.e., 1492) American Indian population of the Western Hemisphere have varied widely. In the 1920s most such estimates were around 50 million; by the 1930s and 1940s scholars aimed considerably lower, around 10 million or slightly more. However, more recent estimates are even higher than those of the 1920s; they approach and sometimes surpass 100 million (Ubelaker, 1976:table 1).

In contrast, estimates of the pre-European population north of the Rio Grande River, in what is now called the United States, Canada, and Greenland, have been more stable and even proportionately much lower. Until the mid-1960s, most estimates were in the neighborhood of 1 million (Ubelaker, 1976:table 1). In 1966, however, Dobyns (1966) estimated a population range of from 9.80 to 12.25 million for 1492. More recent estimates have been considerably lower, despite Dobyns's work, but well above the earlier figure of 1 million. When Ubelaker (1976) summarized tribal population estimates for the new *Handbook of North American Indians*, he estimated a pre-European size of 2,171,125 for this area. Denevan (1976:261) considered Ubelaker's figure to be too low and arbitrarily doubled it to 4.4 million. Recently, Dobyns (1983) estimated that the population north of Mesoamerica may have been as high as 18 million.

If we consider only the area of the contiguous United States, population figures are naturally reduced somewhat. Estimates range from Kroeber's (1939)

720,000 to Dobyns's (1966) 6.65–8.3 million.[1] Mooney's (1928) classic summary figure for the period of initial *extensive* European contact, from 1600 to 1845, depending on the tribe and region in question, is 849,000. Recently, a coworker and I estimated this population at 1,845,180 in the year 1492 (Thornton and Marsh-Thornton, 1981).

Because estimates of total American Indian population of this area vary so widely, estimates for subareas and/or individual tribes are difficult to make. There are a variety of such estimates but no comprehensive ones. One scholar may estimate the size of a particular area or tribe, another that of a different area or tribe. Given wide variation in sizes of the total population estimates, problems arise in comparing them. (See, for example, Thornton, 1978.)

The only areawide estimate that is broken into subarea and tribal estimates is Mooney's (1910a, 1928). However, since his total population estimate is extremely low, figures for specific subareas or tribes are likely to be low as well. Despite this bias, two factors operate in favor of my using Mooney's figures. First, their use provides a consistent source of information and thus enables me to compare relative population sizes between subareas and tribes. Second, Mooney's figures are, as noted, for what he considered the date of first extensive European contact, varying from 1600 for the North and South Atlantic Regions to 1845 for the Central Mountain Region, and not for the date of initial European contact with North America.[2]

Because of these two factors, I chose to use Mooney's estimates to illustrate original subarea differences in pre-European size as well as later declines in American Indian populations. (They were also used for early tribal population estimates in my inter- and intratribal analyses, presented later.)

Regional population sizes from Mooney are shown in Table 4.1, along with his date of first extensive European contact, number of tribes, mean tribal size, and attrition by 1907.

Areas are not of comparable size, so it is not possible to make many comparisons from these data. Mean tribal size may be compared reasonably well, however, although definitional problems of an American Indian "tribe" are present. Nevertheless, the tribal average size seems to vary considerably from region to

---

[1] Dobyns does not provide a separate estimate for the United States. The range reported here was obtained by multiplying his 1930 U.S. nadir population of 332,000 by his depopulation ratios of 20 and 25. However, Driver (1968) argues that this nadir population is too large and too late in time. Of course, the circa 1890 nadir population of as few as 228,000 used here differs greatly from Dobyns's. Both Dobyns's and Driver's nadir populations and dates are discussed in Thornton and Marsh-Thornton (1981).

[2] Mooney (1928), however, considered most tribal populations to have been more or less stable from 1492 until first extensive contact with Europeans; thus his estimates could be considered aboriginal sizes in this regard.

Table 4.1. *Attrition of American Indian tribes in U.S. regions*

Region	Characteristics at European contact				Characteristics in 1907						Tribes extinct or near extinction, %
	Date	Population	No. of tribes	Mean size	Contact size, %	Population	No. of tribes	Mean size	Tribes extinct	Tribes nearing extinction	
North Atlantic	1600	55,600	24	2,317	39.4	21,900	10	2,190	14	6	83.3
South Atlantic	1600	52,200	35	1,491	4.2	2,170	15	145	20	14	97.1
Gulf States	1650	114,400	39	2,933	54.8	62,700	12	5,225	27	4	79.5
Central States	1650	75,300	12	6,275	61.3	46,126	10	4,613	2	1	25.0
Northern Plains	1780	100,800	20	5,040	50.1	50,477	19	2,804	1	1	10.0
Southern Plains	1690	41,000	12	3,417	7.0	2,861	7	409	5	0	41.7
Columbia Region	1780	88,800	95	935	17.4	15,431	83	211	12	40	54.7
Central Mountains	1845	19,300	6	3,217	59.8	11,544	6	1,924	0	0	0
New Mexico and Arizona	1680	72,000	25	2,880	74.8	53,832	19	2,833	6	1	28.0
California	1769	260,000	45	5,778	7.2	18,797	36	696	9	9	40.0
Total		849,000	313			285,838	217		96	66	
Average	1704			2,712	66.3			1,470			57.5

Note: Information on which this table is based was obtained from Mooney (1928), Smith (1928), and Kroeber (1957).

region, from 935 for the Columbia Region to 6,275 for the Central States. As indicated, the overall average was 2,712.

Decline and devastation

Despite much scholarly debate about the size of the pre-European native population of the Western Hemisphere and the U.S. area, no one disputes that native population decline and devastation occurred after European contact. Whatever its aboriginal size, the American Indian population of the contiguous U.S. area declined to as few as 228,000 by circa 1890 (Thornton and Marsh-Thornton, 1981). From this nadir it began to increase again.

Using figures Mooney (1928) supplied for the early 1900s, it is possible to see that decline varied from region to region.[3]

As shown in Table 4.1, tribes of the South Atlantic Region experienced greater devastation than those of any other region. Their size in 1907 was a scant 4.2 percent of what it had been prior to European contact. The magnitude of this decline was approached by tribes of the Southern Plains and California regions, with 1907 populations of 7.0 percent and 7.2 percent of their pre-European size, respectively. Tribes of New Mexico and Arizona fared better than others; their size in the early 1900s was almost 75 percent of what it had been prior to contact with Europeans.

Table 4.1 also gives data on the average size of tribes in 1907. When these are compared with their original populations, variations in change in mean size may be ascertained. As indicated, average tribal size declined by 1,242 people: from 2,712 to 1,470, a decrease of 45.9 percent.

As with magnitude of population decline, changes in average tribal size varied widely. There were decreases of 90.3 percent in the South Atlantic Region and 88.0 percent in both the Southern Plains and California regions, and decreases of only 5.5 percent in the North Atlantic Region and 1.6 percent in New Mexico and Arizona. Tribes in the Gulf States even increased in average size, from 2,933 to 5,225, a gain of 2,292 or 78.1 percent.

Also shown in Table 4.1, more than 97 percent of the pre-European tribes of the South Atlantic Region were either extinct or nearly extinct by the early 1900s. This region was followed by the North Atlantic and Gulf States regions, where more than 83 percent and 79 percent, respectively, of the original tribes became extinct or nearly extinct by 1907. Tribes of the Central Mountains and Northern Plains regions fared relatively well in this regard. By 1907, no tribes in the

---

[3] Figures are by tribe, summed to represent regions; movement of tribes from one region to another does not influence regional totals for the early 1900s.

Table 4.2. *American Indian population in the United States: 1800–1910*

Date	Population
1800	600,000[a]
1820	471,000[b]
1847	383,000[c]
1857	313,000[d]
1870	278,000[e]
1880	244,000[e]
1890	228,000[e]
1900	250,000[e]
1910	279,000[e]

[a] From U.S. Bureau of Indian Affairs (1943), as cited by Hadley (1957:24).
[b] From Morse (1970[1822]:375).
[c] From Schoolcraft (1851–57), as cited by Mallery (1877:341).
[d] From Schoolcraft (1851–57), as cited by Dobyns (1976:55).
[e] From U.S. Bureau of the Census (1915:10).

Central Mountain Region had become extinct. In the Northern Plains Region, 10 percent of the tribes were extinct or nearing extinction, a considerable difference from the overall rate of 57.5 percent.

Population nadir

As shown in Table 4.2, the total aboriginal American Indian population in the United States had declined to about 600,000 by 1800. From this point, it declined in a virtually linear pattern until the circa 1890 population nadir of perhaps only 228,000 (Thornton and Marsh-Thornton, 1981). Since then it has recovered to an enumerated 1,361,869 American Indians in the 1980 census (Swagerty and Thornton, 1982).

For the Far West area, where the Ghost Dances originated, nineteenth-century declines were often more severe. An example may be seen in Table 4.3. From a population size of 260,000 in 1800, representing about 45 percent of the total American Indian population, the California Indian population was reduced to 100,000 by the mid-1800s, then to 30,000 during the next twenty years, then to

Table 4.3. *California Indian population: prehistory–1900*

Date	Population
Prehistory	310,000+
1800	260,000
1834	210,000
1849	100,000
1852	85,000
1856	50,000
1860	35,000
1870	30,000
1880	20,500
1890	18,000
1900	15,500[a]
1907	18,797

Note: Information on which this table was based was obtained from Merriam (1905), Mooney (1928), Cook (1976a), and Thornton (1980). [a]Cook (1976a:70) disagrees with the nadir figure reported here (from Merriam, 1905), arguing that the actual nadir was between some 20,000 and 25,000 and occurred during the decade 1890–1900.

a nadir population of one-half this number at the turn of the century. At this point it represented only 6.2 percent of the total American Indian population.

Reasons for the tremendous American Indian population decline are varied and complex, encompassing high death rates over centuries owing to disease, alcohol, genocide, warfare, population relocation, and destruction of food supplies and ways of life, as Ashburn (1947), Palmer (1948), Hadley (1957), Crosby (1972), Ewers (1973), Unrau (1973), Cook (1973, 1976a, 1976b), and Thornton (1984a, 1984b, in press a) have shown. Fertility rates also declined for these and additional reasons, as Cook (1976a) has discussed regarding American Indians in California.

Without doubt, however, the most important factor was disease. When Europeans came to their new world, they encountered American Indian peoples remarkably free of disease. But they brought with them, for example, smallpox, influenza, diphtheria, cholera, typhus, typhoid fever, bubonic plague, and measles, and possibly also syphilis; when the Europeans later brought the Africans, other deadly diseases such as malaria and yellow fever also came. The imported diseases devastated American Indian populations for four centuries.

A note on the buffalo

Reductions in animal and plant populations closely paralleled the devastation of the American Indian human population following European arrival. This change caused further decline in numbers of American Indians, as well as the further collapse of their societies and cultures. The destruction of the North American buffalo as a source of food and culture for many American Indian peoples is particularly noteworthy.

Much of the destruction took place during the nineteenth century, but it started considerably earlier. During early centuries of European contact, pre-European buffalo populations were reduced significantly from "almost inconceivable numbers in the heyday of the living herds" (Roe, 1970:520), probably about 60 million. The two subspecies of buffalo present then – *Bison bison bison,* the plains buffalo, and *Bison bison athabascae,* the eastern woods buffalo – together covered much of the United States and a portion of Canada and Mexico.

By 1830 the buffalo had been reduced to about 40 million, by more or less "desultory" extermination (see Hornaday, 1889:484–86). Tribes dependent or partially dependent on the buffalo at about this point included the Arapaho, Assiniboin, Blackfoot, Cheyenne, Comanche, Crow, Gros Ventre, Kiowa, Kiowa-Apache, Sarsi, Teton Sioux, Arikara, Hidatsa, Iowa, Kansa, Mandan, Missouri, Omaha, Osage, Oto, Pawnee, Ponca, Santee Sioux, Yankton Sioux, Wichita, Plains Cree, Plains Ojibwa, Shoshone, Caddo, Quapaw, Kutenai, and Flathead; many other tribes, such as the Cherokee, had perhaps been partly dependent in earlier times. (See McHugh, 1972:10.)

The period 1830 to 1888, however, was one of "systematic" extermination. It culminated in the slaughter of the two remaining herds: the southern herd during 1870–74, the northern herd during 1876–83 (see Hornaday, 1889:486–513).

Figures for North American buffalo populations provide graphic documentation of their destruction, as shown in Table 4.4. The nadir year, circa 1895, is remarkably close to the American Indian population nadir, circa 1890. At this date, they were almost extinct. (Since this point, buffalo populations have recovered, as have those of American Indians. In 1970 there were seventeen prominent herds in the United States and Canada, totaling some thirty thousand buffalo [McHugh, 1972:313]; in 1983 there were about fifty thousand buffalo in the United States and Canada [Walker, 1983 (1964):1255].)

Table 4.4. *North American buffalo
population: prehistory–1900*

Date	Population
Prehistory	60,000,000[a]
1800	40,000,000[a]
1850	20,000,000[a]
1865	15,000,000[b]
1870	14,000,000[b]
1875	1,000,000[b]
1880	395,000[b]
1885	20,000[b]
1889	1,091[a]
1895	800[a]
1900	1,024[a]

[a] From Seton (1909).
[b] From Seton (1929).

Conclusions

The population decline of American Indians following centuries of European contact was severe and sometimes decisive, as many tribes did not survive. The decline for the total Indian population in the United States culminated in the late nineteenth century, which was also the time of the Ghost Dance movements. Moreover, tribes in many regions where the Ghost Dance occurred – for example, California and the Southern Plains – suffered particularly in this regard. Therefore the historic demographic context of the Ghost Dance movements seems to provide support for my hypothesis of demographic revitalization.

5. Ghost Dance participation and depopulation

The hypothesis of demographic revitalization may also be tested quantitatively by examining both inter- and intratribal differences in Ghost Dance participation of American Indian peoples. If my reasoning in Chapter 3 is correct, an unfavorable demographic situation of an American Indian tribe at the time of the movements led to that tribe's participation. Conversely, nonparticipation would have indicated a more favorable demographic situation at that time. The same thing may be said of subdivisions within a tribe. This theory, of course, presupposes tribal knowledge of the movements; without such knowledge, nonparticipation has little, if any, meaning.

Variables used for analysis

In order to test my hypothesis in these ways, I have used seven basic variables.

The first variable is, of course, American Indian participation or failure to participate in the Ghost Dance movements, either in 1870 or 1890 (or both), given knowledge of those movements. This is the basic, dependent variable, the object of "explanation." Since both inter- and intratribal analyses are of interest, this variable encompasses a number of American Indian tribes for the intertribal analysis, as well as the subdivisions of a tribe participating in the 1870 dance and a tribe participating in the 1890 dance for the intratribal analysis. The second, third, and fourth variables are demographic ones to explain the differences in participation. The second and third ones are population declines for the group. They encompass declines over a short period, approximately the twenty years prior to the movements, and over a longer period, since extensive European contact with the group first occurred. The fourth variable is the group's absolute population size at the time of the Ghost Dance movements.

Three related "nondemographic" variables also provide subsequent elaborations on findings pertaining to the demographic ones. These are a people's date of extensive European contact, date of actual exposure to the Ghost Dances, and distance from point of Ghost Dance origin.

A detailed discussion of the various procedures whereby these seven variables

28

were measured may be found in Appendix B, along with other methodological considerations. Also contained in Appendix B is a discussion of the statistics (Kendall's) Q, my measure of association, and χ^2 (chi-square), my test of significance. Included there is justification of these statistics and the use of dichotomized variables in the analysis.

Participation and demographic revitalization: intertribal analysis

The effects of the demographic variables are examined first.[1]

Population decline

Population decline of an American Indian tribe is an obvious threat to its demographic survival. Given my reasoning, tribes decreasing in population would seemingly have been more threatened than tribes that were either increasing or maintaining their populations at the time of the Ghost Dance movements and thus would have been more likely to participate in the dances.

This hypothesis is easily tested by looking at a tribe's population declines over the two time periods: first from about twenty years prior to the movements and second from initial European contact until the time of each movement.

Relationships between these population declines and Ghost Dance participation are shown in Table 5.1, reporting values for Q and their significance.

As shown in Table 5.1, for 1870 Ghost Dance tribes there is a positive relationship of .58 between participation and population decline twenty years prior to the movement. For tribes participating in the 1890 dance, the positive relationship is .50. This means that tribes with larger population declines were more likely than those with smaller ones to have participated in the dances. (The actual data are presented in Appendix A in the form of 2×2 contingency tables. Of the forty-one tribes with large declines [over 50 percent], thirty-three participated in 1870 and eight did not; of the twenty-three tribes with smaller declines, twelve participated while eleven did not. Similarly, for the 1890 movement, twenty-seven of thirty-six tribes with larger declines [defined in this instance as over 10 percent] participated; only nineteen of thirty-seven tribes with smaller declines did so.)

Population decline during the twenty years prior to the Ghost Dances is therefore positively related to the tribe's participation in them, but only moderately so. (Q may range from -1.00 to $+1.00$.) Nevertheless, the Q values are significant and the hypothesis is therefore supported.

---

[1] Part of the analysis of the Ghost Dance movements presented in this section was reported earlier (Thornton, 1981, 1982).

Table 5.1. Q *values for relationships between analytical variables*

Analytical variables	1870		1890	
	Q	N	Q	N
Participation and				
20-year decline	.58[a]	64	.50[b]	73
Large tribes	.32	38	.11	36
Small tribes	.82[b]	26	1.00[b]	37
Shasta subdivisions	1.00[b]	8		
Sioux subdivisions			.86[c]	24
Participation and decline				
since European contact	−.03	72	.10	63
Large tribes	−.54[d]	42	−.69[b]	33
Small tribes	.57	29	.79[b]	24
Participation and size	−.72[e]	103	−.82[e]	73
Shasta subdivisions	−.85[d]	9		
Sioux subdivisions			.71[b]	27
Participation and date				
of exposure	.74[c]	103	.89[e]	73
Large tribes	.82[c]	49	.96[e]	36
Small tribes	−.24	54	.48	37
Participation and date				
of European contact	.64[c]	102	.71[e]	72
Large tribes	.70[c]	48	.93[e]	36
Small tribes	.65	54	.24	35
Participation and distance				
from origin	.24	103	.01	73
Size and dates				
of exposure	−.35[d]	103	−.58[d]	73

Note: See Appendix A for contingency tables.
[a] Significant at .02 level.
[b] Significant at .05 level.
[c] Significant at .01 level.
[d] Significant at .10 level.
[e] Significant at .001 level.

When population declines over the longer period are examined, a different picture emerges. As also shown in Table 5.1, participation of tribes in the Ghost Dance movements was not related to population decline from the time of a tribe's first contact with Europeans. This finding does not support the hypothesis.

Size and its effects

Since Ghost Dance participation was only moderately related to twenty year population decline and not at all related to longer-term decline, examining the effects of tribal size on these relationships may provide stronger support for the hypothesis.

My reasoning is that small tribes would have felt population decreases more than would have large tribes because of the greater impact of reduction in the absolute numbers of people remaining. Too, both Ghost Dance movements originated among small bands of Paviotso in western Nevada, it will be recalled, and spread initially among small tribes of that area. This may very well mean that small tribes of the times and places of the movements were more threatened demographically than large tribes and/or more aware of their threatened demographic situations. If so, according to my hypothesis, then small tribes were also more likely to participate than large tribes, irrespective of any population declines at all.

I examine this latter possibility first. As shown in Table 5.1, Ghost Dance participation was very strongly related to tribal size for both movements: For the 1870 dance, the Q of $-.72$ indicates that large tribes were less likely to have participated; for the 1890 dance, the Q of $-.82$ indicates a similar phenomenon. Only four small tribes – the Gabrielino, Mattole, Tubatulabal, and Grande Rhonde Clackamus – failed to participate in 1870; only five small tribes – Jicarilla and Mescalero Apache, Ponca, Jemez Pueblo, and one Ute division – failed to participate in 1890. (See Appendixes A, C, and E.)

Next, the impact of tribal size on the relationships analyzed here between both short- and long-term population decline and Ghost Dance participation can be assessed by ascertaining Q values and their significance separately for small and large tribes.

With this step, we find that whereas participation in each movement originally showed moderate positive correlations with recent population declines, these now disappear for large tribes but become much stronger for small tribes. As shown in Table 5.1, there is no relationship between participation and twenty-year decline for large tribes. There is one for small tribes, however, and the Q of .82 is considerably greater than the overall one of .58. Likewise for the 1890 movement, there is no relationship for large tribes, but there is a "perfect" relationship of 1.00 for small tribes, compared to the overall one of .50. As shown in Appendix A, only two small tribes with large declines did not participate in

1870, the Gabrielino and Mattole. (See also Appendix C.) No small tribe in 1890 with a large decline failed to participate.

A similar reassessment of the overall Qs between the magnitude of tribal population decline from initial contact with Europeans and Ghost Dance participation is possible. Originally, it will be recalled, no relationships existed. As indicated in Table 5.1, however, introducing size has an important effect.

For small tribes of the 1870 movement there is still no relationship between magnitude of population decline and participation. (However, the original nonsignificant Q of $-.03$ is greatly strengthened to a nonsignificant one of .57.) Interestingly, there is now a *negative* relationship between magnitude of decline and participation for the larger tribes: $-.54$.

Small tribes of the 1890 dance now show a relationship of .79. The only small tribe with a large decline that did not participate was the Osage. (See Appendixes A and E.) As with tribes of the 1870 Ghost Dance, the large tribes of the 1890 dance now show a *negative* relationship between magnitude of population decline from European contact and participation. In this instance it is $-.69$.

This analysis supports the hypothesis to a great extent: The impact of size on the original Qs between participation and population decline is considerable. For small tribes, the new relationships are basically as expected; relationships between participation and recent decline increase substantially for small tribes. However, the Q for participation and decline since European contact for small tribes of the 1870 movement is not significant, and statistical support may not be claimed. That the Q does increase greatly is encouraging, of course. The relationships for small tribes of the 1890 Ghost Dance do certainly support the hypothesis.

Explaining the involvement of large tribes

The negative relationships for large tribes between magnitude of population decline from European contact and participation in both Ghost Dances seem an anomaly. Why would large tribes with populations that had declined since European contact tend so strongly not to participate in either movement? Small tribes with similar long-term declines tended to participate, as did those with declines over only a twenty-year period, although large tribes with recent declines showed no pattern.

Analysis of the length of time since European contact may provide insight. Perhaps tribal population loss, if it was experienced over a long period and did not eventually result in a relatively small tribal population, was not actually perceived as threatening tribal survival at the time the movements occurred. Perhaps it even served to reaffirm tribal chances of survival. Since these tribes continued with relatively large numbers (compared to small tribes), they may have been less likely to participate in the Ghost Dances. This explanation would certainly be congruent with my view of the movements as attempts at demographic revitalization.

This interesting possibility may be examined by analyzing relationships between tribal participation and date of contact with Europeans by tribal size. If my reasoning is correct, participation would be positively related to recency of European contact for the larger tribes, particularly because the majority of tribes experienced some population decline during this period.

Table 5.1 shows the two relationships between tribal participation in the Ghost Dance movements and recency of first contact with Europeans. They are .64 for the 1870 dance and .71 for the 1890 one. The vast majority of tribes with more recent contact were participants: Only six of sixty such tribes of the 1870 movement did not participate; only ten of forty-five such tribes of the 1890 movement did not. (See Appendix A.)

These relationships are interesting in their own right, and they support my view of the Ghost Dance movements. They indicate that recency of European contact, and, presumably, recency of threats to demographic survival, influenced tribal participation. Of special interest, however, is the analysis of these two relationships by size of tribe.

As also shown in Table 5.1, participation is not related to date of European contact for small tribes. (However, the Q of .65 for small tribes of the 1870 Ghost Dance is quite close to the overall one for tribes of that movement.) But large tribes of both movements now show strong positive relationships between participation and recency of contact with Europeans, as predicted: For 1870 tribes, Q is .70; for 1890 tribes it is .93.

The findings suggest, then, that tribal perseverance during extended periods of population decline may have reduced perceived threats to demographic survival.

Participation and demographic revitalization: intratribal analysis

Intratribal variations in 1870 and 1890 Ghost Dance participation may provide a further test of the correctness of the hypothesis: If the selected demographic variables were important to participation within a tribe as well as among tribes, then the hypothesis is strengthened considerably.

As detailed in Appendix B, I selected one tribe from each Ghost Dance movement for analysis here: the Shastan peoples of northern California and southern Oregon for the 1870 Ghost Dance movement, and the Sioux of the Northern Plains for the 1890 dance. (See also Appendixes D and F.)

As shown in Table 5.1, the magnitude of recent population decline was strongly and positively associated with participation in the Ghost Dance for both Shastan and Sioux subdivisions: The significant Q values were 1.00 and .86, respectively. Data were not available for the longer period of population decline, as I explain in Appendix B.

Table 5.1 also shows relationships between population size and participation for both Shastan and Sioux subdivisions *but in opposite directions.* For the Shastan, there is a negative relationship of $-.85$, a pattern similar to that found in the intertribal level of analysis. However, for the Sioux, there is a *positive* relationship of .71. That is, the larger Sioux subdivisions were the more likely to have participated in the 1890 dance; the smaller ones were the less likely participants.

These findings for Sioux subdivisions partly contradict earlier ones on the tribal level of analysis and appear to be partly incongruent with the hypothesis of demographic revitalization. This may not necessarily be the case, however.

Sioux involvement in the 1890 Ghost Dance movement was of a different nature than that of most other peoples in either movement, as I discuss in Appendix B. Among the Sioux, the Ghost Dance was a facet of a military confrontation with U.S. government troops and not a totally peaceful movement, as it was for other American Indians. It was also related to the death of Sitting Bull and the genocide at Wounded Knee.

The positive relationship of size and participation may actually make sense in light of this uniqueness. It would be expected that those Sioux subdivisions that had lost more members before the Ghost Dance occurred would be more likely to participate as an effort at demographic revitalization. And this is what happened. However, since Ghost Dance participation also involved a hostile confrontation, it might also be expected that it would be the larger Sioux subdivisions that would resist the U.S. troops and, thus, use the dance: Large numbers are important in fighting a well-armed enemy. Smaller subdivisions, in contrast, would be expected to be less interested – or perhaps merely less willing to participate – in hostilities and in the Ghost Dance movement. This explanation is actually congruent with the hypothesis, as these smaller subdivisions would find participation threatening to their demographic survival: For them survival would be enhanced by avoiding the Ghost Dance altogether, despite its promise to return the dead to life.

A demographic view of diffusion

Though these data and analyses strongly support my hypothesis of demographic revitalization, it is additionally important to ascertain whether Ghost Dance participation was related to tribal proximity to the Ghost Dance movements' site of origin. If so, then it could be argued that participation was only a result of cultural diffusion; groups closer to the site of origin would be more likely participants. (See Driver, 1974, for essays on issues of diffusion.)

To examine this possibility, one can relate tribal distance from the site of origin in western Nevada to tribal participation in the movements. I did so and found no relationship between distance from origin and tribal participation: tribes closer to the Paviotso originators were no more likely to have participated in either movement. The Qs for 1870 and 1890 tribes are not significant, as is shown in Table 5.1.[2]

Although tribal participation was not a product of cultural diffusion, this does not mean that tribal *knowledge* of the movement, was not so; in fact, it undoubtedly was. Tribes closer to the points of origin were surely more likely to hear of them in the first place.

How knowledge of the movements was related to tribal size and participation in the movements will provide further insight into the demography of the movements and perhaps further support for my hypothesis.

Knowledge of the movements

I mentioned in Chapter 1 that the movements spread from a common site of origin but in different directions: the 1870 movement primarily westward, the 1890 movement primarily eastward. I also mentioned that both movements began among small bands of Paviotso, numbering only a few hundred members. Analysis indicates, however, a pronounced pattern of movement toward increasingly larger tribes.

As shown in Table 5.1, relating tribal size with dates of exposure to the movements gives a relationship of $-.35$ between date of exposure and tribal size for the 1870 dance and one of $-.58$ for the 1890 dance. Thus small tribes were more likely to learn of both Ghost Dance movements at an early date than were large tribes.[3]

Knowledge and participation

The temporal pattern of tribal participation may also be examined to ascertain whether tribes learning of the movements at earlier times were more likely to participate than those learning of them at later times.

As indicated in Table 5.1, tribes learning of the movements early were much more likely to participate than those learning of them later: There is a relationship

---

[2] I did not test this hypothesis on the intratribal level, since it is doubtful if differences in distances involved would have really been meaningful.
[3] The same pattern is seen in the proportions of small tribes exposed during different periods. For the 1870 movement, 60 percent of the tribes exposed early were small; only 40 percent of those exposed afterward were small. For the 1890 movement, percentages are 70 percent and 30 percent, respectively.

of .74 between participation and earliness of exposure for the 1870 movement and one of .89 for the 1890 movement.

Only four of fifty-four tribes having early knowledge of the 1870 movement did not participate: the Maidu, Mattole, one Shastan group, and Clackamus at Grande Rhonde. (See Appendixes A and C.) Similarly, only three of thirty-four tribes that learned of the 1890 movement during its first year failed to participate: the Ponca, Santee Sioux, and a group of Ute. (See Appendixes A and E.)

Relationships between participation and dates of exposure to the movements may also be reassessed for large and small tribes separately, to provide further insight. As statistics in Table 5.1 show, tribal size has an important impact on the relationship between participation and date of exposure. There are strong, positive relationships between participation and date of exposure for large tribes but no relationships for small tribes: For the 1870 movement, the relationship is .82; for the 1890 movement, it is .96.

Virtually all large tribes that learned of the 1870 Ghost Dance movement early participated: Nineteen did; only the Maidu and one Shastan group did not. However, fifteen large tribes exposed later did not participate, whereas thirteen did. Dates of exposure had little meaning for small tribes' participation; they participated irrespective of when they learned of the movement. For the thirty-three small tribes exposed early, only the Mattole and Clackamus of Grande Ronde did not participate; of the twenty-one exposed later, only the Gabrielino and Tubatulabal did not participate. (See Appendixes A and C.)

The same pattern is evident for the 1890 Ghost Dance movement. Almost all of the large tribes exposed early participated; of the eleven, only one, the Santee Sioux, did not. However, twenty-one large tribes that were exposed later did not participate, and only four did. For this movement, also, the date of exposure had little meaning for small tribes, which participated overwhelmingly. Of twenty-three that learned of the 1890 dance in its initial year, only the Ponca and a group of Ute did not participate; of fourteen exposed later, only the Jemez Pueblo and Jicarilla and Mescalero Apache did not participate. (See Appendixes A and E.)

Conclusions

The demographic and related characteristics examined here were important to American Indian participation in the Ghost Dance movements of the nineteenth century, both inter- and intratribally. And considerable support for my hypothesis may be claimed.

Population declines were associated with this participation, as originally thought. However, their importance seems to have been less than that of size per se. Size influenced these relationships and was highly related to participation, both inter- and intratribally.

The participation of large tribes in both Ghost Dance movements required more complex explanation. The perseverance of these tribes over long periods of European contact fostered nonparticipation in the movements. Their participation was influenced strongly by the dates they learned of the movements, a finding which suggests that the movements may have been stronger in their earlier years, so that large tribes became caught up in them.

For small tribes, whose survival was more threatened in an absolute sense, dates of exposure made little difference. They were receptive to the Ghost Dances no matter when they learned of them. Mooney (1910b:173) noted this same phenomenon in an address to the Nebraska Historical Society: "The smaller tribes, having nearly lost their own old forms, were glad to take up the new ritual."

6. Participation and population recovery

Each Ghost Dance movement lasted only a few years, but this does not mean that each did not have lasting effect on American Indian peoples. As mentioned in Chapter 1, each movement actually became institutionalized as a religion or religious cult in some tribes, and three cults developed from the 1870 Ghost Dance: the Earth Lodge Cult, the *Bole-Maru,* and the Big Head Cult. These cults persisted well beyond the movement, into the present century. The 1890 Ghost Dance continues as religion and ceremony today.

In Chapter 4 I gave a nadir figure for the total U.S. American Indian population: about 228,000 circa 1890. After that time the American Indian population began to increase gradually, then more sharply, until by 1980 it approached 1.4 million. Considerable tribal variations in recovery are present: Populations of some tribes increased while others decreased, even to extinction. (See Thornton, 1984b, in press b.) Conceivably, tribal involvement in either Ghost Dance might have influenced subsequent population change.

Various speculations here are possible: Were participants more successful in reversing population trends and achieving demographical revitalization? Were they less successful? Were both participants and nonparticipants equally successful or unsuccessful?

One might expect the latter to be the true situation: that Ghost Dance participation had absolutely no impact on the subsequent population histories of American Indian peoples in question. Participant and nonparticipant tribes were equally likely to have subsequent population gains or losses, as there is no reason to expect the movements to influence population increase or decrease. Surely no American Indian dead were returned to life.

It could be argued, however, that participant tribes might show less gain than others, because their efforts were directed toward population recovery by means of the Ghost Dance rather than by, say, increasing food supply. It could also be argued that participation might for one reason or another have increased the death rate. Some Sioux were killed, directly or indirectly, as a result of their involvement. Many Indians believed that individual participants would die. This belief was widespread in California in the 1870s. Referring to both Ghost Dances, a

38

Navajo man indicated: "A few years after the first time I heard this [1870] there was an epidemic of measles and a great many people died. A few years after the second time [1890] an epidemic of mumps killed a great number of people" (Hill, 1944:526). Some American Indians even held the Ghost Dances to be somehow responsible for their overall population decrease (Du Bois, 1939:4).

Alternatively, tribes participating might have had more population gains than ones not participating. Participation might have been an important recognition that survival was threatened; this recognition, in turn, might have led to other efforts to assure survival. Surely, participation would have meant greater contact with other tribes and increased opportunities for mate selection, which was probably of special importance to small tribes.

Whatever the speculations, the facts are easily examined.

Variables used for analysis

I study the relationship between Ghost Dance participation and subsequent population change using five basic variables. The first, of course, are Ghost Dance participation and population change itself, ascertained for both twenty and forty years after the movements. As an elaboration on this analysis, I use the additional variables of changes in proportion of full-bloods in the population, both twenty and twenty to forty years after the movements. (See Appendix B for the measurement of these.)

Population change and participation

The relationships of population increase or decrease twenty years and forty years after each movement and tribal participation are shown in Table 6.1.

For 1870 Ghost Dance tribes, there are relationships between participation and population change twenty and forty years later of .82 and .78, respectively; for 1890 tribes, these relationships are both .63. Participating tribes in both movements were therefore more likely to have increased populations twenty as well as forty years after each movement.

Further, contingency tables in Appendix A show that, overwhelmingly, tribes with population increases over both periods were participants, whereas those with decreases may or may not have been. Of thirty-seven tribes in 1870 with twenty-year increases, only the Lusieno, Navajo, and Klickitat did not participate in the Ghost Dance; of twenty-four tribes in 1890 with twenty-year increases, only four did not participate: the Yankton and Santee Sioux, Navajo, and Zuni. Of twenty 1870 tribes with forty-year increases, only the Navajo did not participate in this Ghost Dance; of twenty-nine tribes in 1890 with forty-year

Table 6.1. Q *values for relationships between analytical variables*

Analytical variables	1870		1890	
	Q	N	Q	N
Participation and				
subsequent population change				
20 years later	.82[a]	83	.63[b]	67
40 years later	.78[c]	83	.63[b]	57
Subsequent population change				
and change in % of full-blood				
members				
20 years later	−.79[a]	75	.51[c]	62
20–40 years later	−.72[a]	74	.47[d]	54
Participation and change				
in % of full-blood members				
20 years later	−.64[c]	103	.67[e]	70
20–40 years later	−.52[c]	91	.87[a]	71

Note: See Appendix A for contingency tables.
[a] Significant at .001 level.
[b] Significant at .02 level.
[c] Significant at .05 level.
[d] Significant at .10 level.
[e] Significant at .01 level.

increases, only six did not participate: the Osage, Jemez and Keres Pueblo, Hopi, Zuni, and Navajo. (See Appendixes C, E, G, and H.)

As reported earlier, participant tribes tended to be small, with sharply decreasing populations, whereas nonparticipants tended to be large, with increasing or less sharply decreasing populations. The Ghost Dance movements marked the point at which these trends were reversed.

Only three variables account for the numerical change of a population: births, deaths, and migration. A population increases when gains through these factors outnumber losses; it decreases when the reverse is true. Tribes participating in the 1870 and 1890 Ghost Dances thus had total gains through births, deaths, and migrations; this was not necessarily the case for nonparticipating tribes.

Population change is also dependent upon how a population is defined over time; changes in definition may result in changes in size. Such changes were important in the American Indian population during the period.

Mixed-blood, full-blood, and population change

Since early contact between American Indians and Europeans, there have been mixed offspring. The status of these mixed-bloods has often been problematic: Sometimes they have been considered American Indian, sometimes not.

Early treaties between Indian tribes and the U.S. government sometimes provided specifically for so-called mixed-bloods; for example, the Treaty with the Sauk and Foxes, etc., 1830; the Treaty with the Ponca, 1858; the Treaty with the Kansa Tribe, 1859; and the Treaty with the Omaha, 1865 (all in Institute for the Development of Indian Law, n.d.a); and also the unratified Treaty between the United States and the Blackfoot Nation of Indians, etc., November 16, 1865; the Agreement with the Indians of the Fort Belknap Indian Reservation in Montana, 1895; and the Agreement with the Indians of the Blackfeet Indian Reservation in Montana, 1895 (all in Institute for the Development of Indian law, n.d.b).

Generally, mixed-bloods who accepted tribal ways of life were welcomed, whereas those who preferred non-Indian ways were not. This distinction is indicated, for example, in an 1858 treaty between the United States and the Ponca: "The Ponca being desirous of making provision for their half-breed relatives, it is agreed that those who prefer and elect to reside among them shall be permitted to do so, and be entitled to and enjoy all the rights and privileges of members of the tribe" (Institute for the Development of Indian Law, n.d.a:67). Mixed-bloods could choose, however, not to live among their fellow tribesmen on reservation areas, as the unratified 1865 Treaty between the United States and Blackfoot Nation of Indians indicates (Institute for the Development of Indian Law, n.d.b:72).

During the population recovery of American Indians from the 1890s to today, an increasing amount of admixture between American Indians and other U.S. populations has occurred. Population change in the two time periods following the Ghost Dance movements may be looked at in this light. Some 57 percent of individuals enumerated as American Indians in the 1910 census (U.S. Bureau of the Census, 1915:31) were enumerated as full-blood; 35 percent were listed as mixed-blood; and the degree of Indian blood of more than 8 percent was not specified. In the 1930 census (U.S. Bureau of the Census, 1937:75), only 46 percent of American Indians were enumerated as full-blood; 42 percent were given as mixed-blood; and the degree of Indian blood of 11 percent was not specified. It seems that an important part of American Indian population recovery during this period was through a "biological" migration of non-Indian genes into the American Indian population.

The path of migration was not one-way, however. Whereas non-Indians contributed genes to American Indians, so have American Indians contributed genes to non-Indians. Although in 1980 there were slightly fewer than 1.4 million American Indians, 6 to 7 million Americans had some degree of American Indian ancestry (U.S. Bureau of the Census, 1983:table 2). Just as American Indians have gained population through mixing with non-Indians, so have they lost.

Changes in population and "blood"

Since American Indian population changes are associated with changes in relative proportions of Indian and non-Indian "blood," the differential population growth of tribes after the two Ghost Dance movements may be looked at in these terms.

As shown in Table 6.1, population decrease or increase for twenty years following the Ghost Dance was associated with change in proportion of full-blood members. Relationships between population increase and decrease in proportion of full-blood members were in opposite directions, however: There is a negative relationship of −.79 for tribes of the 1870 Ghost Dance, and there is a positive relationship of .51 for tribes of the 1890 Ghost Dance.

The same pattern is evident for population changes twenty to forty years after the Ghost Dance. There is a negative relationship of −.72 for tribes of the 1870 movement; there is a positive relationship of .47 for tribes of the 1890 movement.

The findings for tribes of the 1890 movement might be expected, in light of the relation between the increase in the total American Indian population of the United States and the increase in the amount of white admixture during the same period. Findings for the tribes of the 1870 movement contrast sharply, however. For these tribes, population increase was associated with maintaining the full-blood segment.

If Ghost Dance participation was associated with these changes in the proportion of full-blood tribal members, then a basis might exist for explaining how participation influenced population change.

Relationships between participation and change in full-blood tribal members are shown in Table 6.1. For the 1870 movement, the Q of −.64 indicates that participation was negatively related to twenty-year change in full-blood members; rather, it was associated with maintenance of the full-blood population. In contrast, the Q for the relationship for the tribes of the 1890 Ghost Dance is a positive one of .67; Ghost Dance participation was associated with a twenty-year increased admixture of non-Indian blood.

The same patterns are evident for the period of twenty to forty years after the movements: a negative relationship of −.52 for tribes of the 1870 Ghost Dance, a positive relationship of .87 for tribes of the 1890 Ghost Dance.

Impact of participation

How participation in the Ghost Dance movements influenced subsequent population changes in opposite ways remains a question. Differences between groupings of tribes involved in the two Ghost Dances may provide a partial explanation, as may the social meaning of the movements to the tribes and the biological migration between Indian and non-Indian population segments.

Tribal differences between the movements

By and large, American Indians involved in the 1870 Ghost Dance had not experienced extensive European contact as early as those involved in the 1890 Ghost Dance. When such contacts were made, however, these tribes soon suffered population reductions so drastic that for the most part, by the 1870 movement, they were remnants of their former states. (See Appendix C.) At this same time, tribal lands were overrun by Europeans. Few reservation systems had been established for Indian tribes: Only one-third of the tribes of the 1870 dance were on reservations. The others were left basically to wander as best they could.

The situation of tribes of the 1890 Ghost Dance movement was in sharp contrast. They had had a longer period of European contact. (See Appendix E.) More importantly, by the 1890 Ghost Dance period an elaborate reservation system had been established. Almost all the tribes of the 1890 Dance were on reservations.

Cook (1943:33–34) writes of these differences:

Over most of the United States the survivors of the Indian population have been restricted to reservations or otherwise subjected to artificial constraint. Hence any natural tendency to move about has been sharply inhibited. The State of California has, however, constituted an exception and has provided an opportunity to observe what an Indian group would do if left largely to its own initiative. The causes of this anomalous situation are clear. The first lies in the fact that the majority of California Indians were never reservationized but were left to merge as best they might with the American civilization which surrounded them. The second factor lies in the peculiar manner in which the state was settled. From 1848 to 1860 the entire coastal region was suddenly overrun by whites who, to be sure, killed and starved large numbers of the natives but who left the survivors to persist in their ancestral habitat. The aborigines were thus submerged, rather than expelled or exterminated. The third factor was the very strong Spanish-Mexican tradition which persisted long after the American conquest. This tradition, strongly reinforced by the Catholic clergy, envisaged the Indian as an integral, even if subordinate, component of the social organism itself, rather than as an enemy to be segregated in isolation.

Dynamics of population increase

Tribal population increase apparently occurred oppositely, therefore, for the two groupings. For tribes of the 1870 movement, with little reservation basis and hence few physical boundaries, population increase occurred through maintaining the full-bloods rather than by admixture with Europeans. Population decrease occurred because of opposite conditions. Given their nonreservation status and the lack of boundaries between the tribes and Europeans, offspring of mixed marriages may have joined the general population of California and other states and not maintained Indian identity (at least for census purposes).

Conversely, tribes of the 1890 Ghost Dance with reservation bases had population increases from admixture with non-Indians. Given reservation boundaries, offspring of mixed marriages were more likely to maintain Indian identity (again, at least for census purposes).

Resulting differences in these population processes may be seen in percentages of full-bloods in the two tribal groupings forty years after the movements.

Overall, there is little difference: 1870 Ghost Dance tribes had 67 percent full-blood members in 1910; 1890 Ghost Dance tribes were 64 percent full-blood in 1930. However, distinguishing tribes that participated from those that did not sharpens these differences. Participating tribes in the 1870 dance had 71 percent full-blood, and nonparticipating tribes had 55 percent; participating tribes in the 1890 Ghost Dance had 63 percent, and nonparticipating tribes had 66 percent (U.S. Bureau of the Census, 1915:table 51, 1937:table 14).

Thus participating tribes of the 1870 dance had a higher percentage of full-blood members forty years afterward than did nonparticipating ones; they also had a higher percentage than participating tribes of the 1890 dance forty years after that movement. Participating tribes of 1890, however, had a lower percentage of full-bloods forty years later than did nonparticipating tribes.

Therefore it seems that American Indian tribes participating in the two movements increased their populations through opposite dynamics: Those of the 1870 Ghost Dance were increased by a process of racial *exclusiveness,* those of 1890 by a process of racial *inclusiveness.*

Group solidarity and the movements

Participation in the movements was, however, associated with both exclusive and inclusive processes of American Indian population increase. This may be explained by the solidarity function of social movements and by the biological migrations of American Indians.

Tribal participation in the Ghost Dance movements may well have resulted in the creation of enhanced tribal solidarity; such social movements have strong integrative functions, as Worsley (1957) has shown for social movements throughout the world. This would have been particularly important in periods of population growth.

Increased solidarity, in turn, may have resulted in increased distinctions between American Indian and European populations. For tribes participating in the

1870 movement, who had no elaborate reservation systems, solidarity served to maintain tribal boundaries and keep full-bloods within the tribe; mixed-bloods may have migrated to the general non-Indian population. For participating tribes of the 1890 movement, with extensive reservation systems, solidarity served to keep mixed-bloods within tribal boundaries; tribes not participating may have lost this element to the general population.

Conclusions

It is thus possible to say that the two Ghost Dance movements actually "worked" – not, of course, by returning deceased American Indian populations to life, but by strengthening tribal identity and distinctions between American Indian and European populations. These in turn served to strengthen tribal boundaries, which restricted migrations out of the tribe during population growth. Not participating did nothing to strengthen boundaries at a crucial time in a tribe's population history and thus did not encourage full-bloods of the 1870 movement or mixed-bloods of the 1890 movement to remain within tribes. Likely important in this process was whether or not an American Indian group had a reservation base.

7. A summary, a conclusion, some implications

To finalize my research on the American Indian Ghost Dances, I offer here a summary and a conclusion, along with some implications of findings.

A summary

As discussed in Chapter 2, scholars have suggested cultural, social, even psychological, explanations of the Ghost Dance movements among American Indian peoples of the 1870s and 1890s. I suggest another though not necessarily contradictory explanation, one derived both from the study of other social movements and from the central expressed objective of the Ghost Dances. It is my view that both Ghost Dances were deliberate efforts by American Indian peoples to accomplish their demographic revitalization. In other words, they sought to assure survival as physical peoples through regaining population – bringing the dead to life – by performing the Ghost Dance cermonies.

I tested my view, as expressed in a hypothesis of demographic revitalization, in three ways.

First, I tested it by examining the historic demographic context of the movements. I discovered that both Ghost Dances occurred more or less in geographic areas in which there had been severe American Indian population losses: The first Ghost Dance was centered in California, after the decimation of California Indians; the second, more persuasive, Ghost Dance coincided almost exactly with the total American Indian population nadir; further, actual participants in both movements tended to live in the subareas with the greatest population losses. This all suggests a very close linkage between American Indian population losses and the social occurrence of the Ghost Dance movements.

More important, perhaps, was my quantitative examination of the differential participation of Indian groups in the movements, using selected demographic and related variables. Results here seem dramatic. Both population change and population size were related to participation on inter- and intratribal levels of analysis. However, size was surely the more important variable. Size was related strongly to participation overall: negatively related to the participation of tribes

46

in both Ghost Dances and to Shastan subdivisions in the 1870 movement; positively related to the participation of Sioux subdivisions in the 1890 movement – perhaps an anomaly owing to the particular circumstances of the Sioux at that time.

Size also influenced the relationships between participation and population changes, particularly changes over a long time period. Seemingly, small tribes felt the impact of depopulation more than did large tribes, perhaps because population losses were more visible and of more immediate impact within them. The participation of large tribes in the movements seemed more complicated. Their participation was strongly influenced by both the time of initial contact with Europeans and the time of exposure to the Ghost Dances. The former's influence may be explained by tribal survival over extended depopulation; the latter's influence may be explained by the movements' greater strength in their earlier years.

I have additionally shown that tribal participation was associated with positive demographic results; that is, participating tribes were more likely to have population increases following the Ghost Dances. Although the increases resulted from different processes for the tribal groupings of the two dances, both population increases probably occurred because the movements fostered tribal solidarity and thus restricted biological emigration. (Group rituals such as the Ghost Dances seem important mechanisms for generating solidarity in tribal societies.) Restricted emigration fostered population growth within the tribe by maintaining the full-bloods for tribes of the 1870 movement and mixed-bloods for tribes of the 1890 movement.

A conclusion

The Ghost Dances have often been as ''a hysterical reaction to the disorganization, frustration, and deprivation experienced by . . . Indians after their series of last-ditch battles'' (Kehoe, 1968:302). To the contrary, it appears to me that the movements were deliberate responses to threatening situations, responses that probably made sense to the Indians involved. As Overholt (1974:46) has commented on the 1890 Dance,

We may be tempted to write of Wovoka's millennarianism as a fore-doomed and ''irrational'' response to the crises of White domination. . . . But we should be willing to entertain the notion that for the people who heard this message . . . calling on the supernatural for aid in throwing off this grave menace must have been, in terms of their culture, an essential ''rational'' act.

As I have indicated, when the movements' predicted events did not occur, American Indians often either lost interest and stopped participating, as Gayton

(1930) has maintained for tribes of the 1870 dance, or developed the movement into a religion, as Mooney (1896:927) and Kehoe (1968) have shown for tribes of the 1890 dance.

Likewise, peoples participating in the 1870 Ghost Dance generally did not join the movement of 1890, perhaps because they had discovered earlier that it "failed to bring back the dead" (Gayton, 1930:62). And, too, in many cases demographic situations had changed in the intervening period (Bean and Vane, 1978:670–72).

My quantitative analysis shows that tribes more in need of population gains were participants, while those in less need of such gains were nonparticipants. My analysis also shows that it was the larger and not the smaller Sioux subdivisions that particpated in the 1890 dance, with its military implications; of course, the larger Sioux groups stood more of a chance than the smaller against government troops.

Both my analysis of the literature and my research findings suggest, then, that the movements were deliberate and "rational" from the American Indians' perspective, not hysterical. (See also DeMallie, 1982.)

Some implications

My research has implications for the occurrence of revitalization and other social movements as well as for the particular form they may take. (See Jenkins, 1983, especially pp. 530–32, and Olzak, 1983, for discussions of why social movements form.)

The deliberate nature of participation in the dances argues in support of the rational view of social movements, as articulated by the "resource mobilization" theorists. However, the demographic devastation of the American Indians at the time the dances occurred and the findings on differential participation support the "relative deprivation" view of such social movements. (See Traugott, 1978.) Integration of these approaches seems clearly needed. (See Klandermans, 1984, and Killian, 1984, for current research studies on these and related issues.)

In other research (Thornton, 1984c, 1985), I have showed a relationship between social and cultural deprivations imposed on nineteenth-century Cherokee society and the occurrence of Cherokee revitalization movements. Both demographic decimations preceding the Ghost Dances and the sociocultural deprivations of the Cherokee, I argued in that research, may be considered instances whereby tribal boundaries were in danger of breaking down. The boundaries may have been demographic ones, as examined here in the study of the Ghost Dances, or they may have been social and cultural ones, as examined in my studies of the Cherokee.

This conclusion implies, then, a parsimonious hypothesis that may possibly explain, at least partially, attempted revitalization movements: *Revitalization efforts are likely to occur when group boundaries are in danger of dissolution.* This hypothesis may be considered similar to Erikson's (1966) argument that the Salem witch-hunts were attempts to strengthen dissolving social boundaries and to Tilly's claims regarding "proactive," "competitive," and "reactive" social movements expressed in *From Mobilization to Revolution* (1978).

Also, I should emphasize that I focus on the occurrence of revitalization attempts, not on whether the attempts proved ultimately successful or not. (Champagne, 1983, for example, has examined the latter aspect. See also Thornton, 1985, and Champagne, 1985, for further discussion of this issue.)

Revitalization and other movements do assume different forms, furthermore. For example, Barber (1941) asserts that nonviolent messianic movements such as the Ghost Dances represent one of several responses to deprivation, others being armed rebellion, physical violence, depopulation, and moral depression. My findings also have implications for the form of social movements.

It will be recalled that the Ghost Dances were generally nonviolent for most American Indian participants. Among the Sioux, however, the 1890 dance took on a militaristic nature and was related to their conflict with the U.S. government. Moreover, it was the larger Sioux subdivisions that participated, not the smaller ones, as was the case with the Shastan.

It may therefore be that militaristic movements are more appealing to larger native populations and nonviolent, perhaps even mystical, movements more appealing to small and declining populations.[1]

Another implication of my research should be noted. The American Indian peoples studied represent wide variations. The two separate groupings of tribes – for the 1870 and for the 1890 movements – were separated by twenty years and many miles. They ranged from small, scattered bands of Paviotso to large divisions of the Sioux to the Navajo. Such distinct peoples as these and the Taos Pueblo, the Yuki, the Ojibwe, and others included in my analysis also exhibited vast cultural and social differences.

Sociocultural differences have sometimes been used to explain differences in Ghost Dance participation. For example, as I have mentioned, Hill (1944) explained Navajo nonparticipation in the 1890 dance as a result of Athabaskan fear of the dead.[2]

---

[1] This idea was first suggested to me by Tony Paredes in response to an earlier report of part of my study. See also Paredes and Plante (1982:21–22).

[2] Other factors could have also been involved. Thomas (1961:165), for example, shows the particular nature of the Cherokee inhibiting movements: "Cherokee culture does not allow for a prophet no matter how much stress the society is under. One man just does not initiate action this way."

In my quantitative analysis, certain peoples constantly presented exceptions: the Jicarilla and Mescalero Apaches, Navajo, Pueblo, Ponca, Sioux, Ute, Clackamus, Gabrielino, and Mattole. Some exceptions surely may be explained in social and cultural terms. For instance, the Apache who did not participate are Athabaskan peoples and share a fear of the dead with the Navajo; many also had a long history of guerilla warfare prior to the Ghost Dance movements. Also, the only Pueblo group accepting the Ghost Dance was the Taos, the northernmost Pueblo people and the one closest linguistically and culturally to the participating Southern Plains tribes: Their pueblo was even a trade center between the Southwest and the Plains.

Consequently, I do not imply that other explanations of the Ghost Dance movements are unimportant, only that demographic ones are important.

American Indian population decline resulted generally in considerable social and cultural "loss." Dobyns (1983:328) observes: "A good deal of social science research has noted that a growing population generates increasingly complex social organization. It must be recognized that population declines resulted in simplification of aboriginal Native American social organization."

Social and cultural restorations were also objectives of the movements, but they would occur only through demographic revitalization: The dead would return and bring former ways of life with them.

In traditional Pawnee society, for example, important knowledge was passed directly from one individual to another and "only direct learning . . . sanctioned use and demonstration" (Lesser, 1933:113). By the 1890s the Pawnee had lost their traditional ways of life without any prospect of regaining them, since the holders of such knowledge were all dead. The promise of the Ghost Dance movement of this time was that these dead would return and bring their knowledge: "Indian ways were not gone, never to be recovered. Indian ways were coming back. Those who had lived before in the 'golden age' were still carrying on old ceremonies, old dances, old performances, and old games in the beyond. They were coming back; they were bringing the old ways and the buffalo. Dance, dance, dance" (Lesser, 1933:112).

> The spirit host is advancing, they say.
> The spirit host is advancing, they say.
> They are coming with the buffalo, they say.
> They are coming with the buffalo, they say.
> They are coming with the (new) earth, they say.
> They are coming with the (new) earth, they say.
> – Kiowa Ghost Dance song

Technical appendixes

Appendix A. *Contingency tables for* Q *and* χ^2 *values*

Analytical variables:[a] dichotomy	Dichotomy		1870 participation (nos. of tribes)		1890 participation (nos. of tribes)	
	1870	1890	Yes	No	Yes	No
Twenty-year decline						
Large decline	50%+	10%+	33	8	27	9
Small decline	50%−	10%−	12	11	19	18
Large tribes						
Large decline			13	6	5	9
Small decline			10	9	9	13
Small tribes						
Large decline			20	2	22	0
Small decline			2	2	10	5
Shastan subdivisions						
Large decline	50%+		4	0		
Small decline	50%−		1	3		
Sioux subdivisions						
Large decline		20%+			13	2
Small decline		20%−			3	6
Decline since contact with Europeans						
Large decline	80%+	50%+	30	11	19	12
Small decline	80%−	50%−	23	8	18	14
Large tribes						
Large decline			8	8	2	11
Small decline			20	6	10	10
Small tribes						
Large decline			22	3	17	1
Small decline			3	1	3	3

51

Appendix A. (*cont.*)

Analytical variables:[a] dichotomy	Dichotomy		1870 participation (nos. of tribes)		1890 participation (nos. of tribes)	
	1870	1890	Yes	No	Yes	No
Population size						
Large	200+	845+	32	17	14	22
Small	200−	845−	50	4	32	5
Shastan subdivisions						
Large size	200+		1	3		
Small size	200−		4	1		
Sioux subdivisions						
Large size		1,000+			11	3
Small size		1,000−			5	8
Distance from origin						
Near	300− mi	800− mi	49	10	24	14
Far	300+ mi	800+ mi	33	11	22	13
Date of exposure						
Early	1871−	1889	50	4	31	3
Late	1872+	1890+	32	17	15	24
Large tribes						
Early exposure			19	2	10	1
Late exposure			13	15	4	21
Small tribes						
Early exposure			31	2	21	2
Late exposure			19	2	11	3
Date of first European contact						
Recent contact	1800+	1700+	54	6	35	10
Late contact	1800−	1700−	28	14	10	17
Large tribes						
Recent contact			23	5	13	7
Late contact			9	11	1	15
Small tribes						
Recent contact			31	1	22	2
Late contact			19	3	9	2

Appendix A. (*cont.*)

	1870 exposure (nos. of tribes)		1890 exposure (nos. of tribes)	
	1870–71	1872–77	1889	1890–92
Population size				
Large	21	28	11	25
Small	33	21	23	14
	1870 participation (nos. of tribes)		1890 participation (nos. of tribes)	
	Yes	No	Yes	No
Subsequent population size				
20-year increase	34	3	20	4
20-year decrease	29	17	23	20
40-year increase	19	1	23	6
40-year decrease	44	19	14	14
	1870 full-blood decline (nos. of tribes)		1890 full-blood decline (nos. of tribes)	
	16%+	16%−	21%+	21%−
20-year increase	10	31	11	12
20-year decrease	25	9	9	30
	11%+	11%−	2.5%+	2.5%−
20–40-year increase	15	32	25	10
20–40-year decrease	20	7	9	10
	1870 participation (nos. of tribes)		1890 participation (nos. of tribes)	
	Yes	No	Yes	No
Full-blood decline				
20-year				
Large	37	21	24	5
Small	40	5	20	21
20–40-year				
Large	37	16	41	9
Small	34	4	5	16

[a]Data in this table were obtained from Appendixes C through H.

Appendix B. *Some considerations of methodology*

My quantitative study of the Ghost Dance movements and their effects involved several methodological procedures, as discussed in this appendix.

Sources of data

First, measuring the analytical variables to be used required the attainment of various types of data.

Participation

In studying participation in the Ghost Dance movements, I had first to determine which groups of American Indians knew of them, and when. Nonparticipation had little, if any, meaning if a group did not know about the movements, as I have indicated. Therefore I needed data about Ghost Dance knowledge initially. Data were then required about which tribes did or did not participate in either movement.

The information I used to establish which of hundreds of nineteenth-century American Indian peoples were aware of either movement and which participated in either or both was obtained from published, primarily scholarly, accounts of the Ghost Dances. Such accounts typically discuss the spread of the movements from tribe to tribe. They also typically contain information about tribes knowing of the movements but not participating. For each of the two Ghost Dances, there is a more or less standard scholarly reference: Du Bois's *The 1870 Ghost Dance* (1939) and Mooney's *The Ghost-Dance Religion and the Sioux Outbreak of 1890* (1896). These works were my starting points for the respective movements; however, they were supplemented by other accounts.

Tribes of the 1870 Ghost Dance movement. My list of American Indian peoples aware of the 1870 movement was established from Du Bois (1939); actual participation was then determined from the same source. I next expanded and refined the list using data from Kroeber (1925), Spier (1927), and Gayton (1930), particularly, but also Hill (1944), Nash (1955 [1937]), Jorgensen (1972), and Heizer (1978). Dates of first participation or, for nonparticipants, of first knowledge of the movement were ascertained from these same sources.

Establishing tribal units for analysis was an additional task. The appropriate unit of an American Indian people – that is, tribe, subtribe, band, or group – is an old, extremely complicated problem.[1] It is exacerbated by the reservation

---

[1] See U.S. Bureau of the Census (1915) for a discussion of these problems, especially the comparability of enumerated American Indian populations around the turn of the century. See also Fried

system whereby tribes were divided and/or combined with other tribes. Given interest in population variables, I decided generally to avoid subtribal distinctions and close geographical designations in arriving at a final list of tribes, because these could impose artificial "smallness." However, I typically followed authorities such as Du Bois when there were indications of distinct tribal differences, like those regarding the Pomo; geographical separateness, as in the case of the Paviotso; and/or variations in participation, as with the Alsea.

One hundred three American Indian peoples had knowledge of the 1870 Ghost Dance movements. (See Appendix C.) I defined participation as a tribe performing the Ghost Dance ceremony, as opposed to only some tribal members joining a ceremony of another tribe: Eighty-two tribes were participants; twenty-one tribes were nonparticipants. Dates of initial participation in the 1870 movement, or of first knowledge of it for nonparticipants, range from very early 1870 to sometime between 1874 and 1877.

The Shastan of the 1870 Ghost Dance. I imposed three data requirements on participant tribes of the 1870 Ghost Dance in selecting one for intratribal analysis: First, I needed information about which subdivisions did and did not participate; second, given this information, I needed a number of subdivisions with differences in participation to make analysis possible and meaningful; and, third, I wanted demographic data on the subdivisions for different periods. The Shastan peoples met these requirements, though only limited data were available.

Shastan peoples encompassed several linguistically similar American Indian groups, generally divided into the Shasta per se and three minor groups, the Konomihu, Okwanuchu, and New River Shasta (Silver, 1978:211).[2] Tribal location at first European contact was what is now far northern central California and southern central Oregon.

The Shastan peoples' initial contact with Europeans was in the early 1800s, when fur trappers visited the territory. At this time the Shastan were estimated to number about three thousand: two thousand Shasta proper and about one thousand for other groups combined. By 1850 many whites, particularly gold miners, had invaded their land, and the entire Shastan population at this point had shrunk to fewer than two thousand.

From 1850 onward, the Shastan experienced drastic changes. All of the Shasta

---

(1975) for a discussion of "tribe"; Hall (1983) for a discussion of the effects of state societies on the boundaries of nonstate societies; and Wolf (1982) for a discussion of the deformation of "native" group boundaries in Europe.

[2] Earlier scholars included the Achumawi and Atsugewi with the Shastan peoples. According to Silver (1978:211), however, linguistic studies done in the 1950s indicated that this inclusion is inappropriate.

proper in Oregon and California were involved to some extent in the Rogue River wars (Beckham, 1971; Silver, 1978:212), and by the mid-1850s they were located on Grande Ronde and Siletz reservations in Oregon (Silver, 1978:212), having suffered heavy losses (Beckham, 1971:144–45). The other divisions, the Konomihu, Okwanuchu, and New River Shasta, lived at the southern edge of Shastan territory, entirely in California. They apparently did not participate in the wars, since they were some distance from the hostilities in Oregon, but by 1855 their numbers barely exceeded five hundred.

The Shasta per se came in contact with the Ghost Dance movement of 1870, embraced it and its derivations, and became active in transmitting the movement to other Indians (Du Bois, 1939:2). Konomihu, New River, and Okwanuchu divisions apparently were aware of this Ghost Dance movement through contact with the Shasta per se; however, there is no indication that any of them actually participated.

I divided Shastan peoples into subdivisions and locations on the basis of information in Du Bois (1939), Beckham (1971), and Silver (1978). Shasta proper were divided into Oregon and California groups, the Oregon Shasta then into those on the Grande Ronde and Siletz reservations and around Jacksonville, and the California Shasta then into Klamath River, Scott Valley, and Shasta Valley Shasta. Other Shastan peoples were divided into the Konomihu, Okwanuchu and New River Shasta. Each of the nine subdivisions was then classified for participation using information from Du Bois (1939) and Silver (1978). (See Appendix D.)

Tribes of the 1890 Ghost Dance movement. Establishing knowledge of and participation in the 1890 Ghost Dance proceeded somewhat differently than for the 1870 movement. There is an extensive, detailed body of scholarly literature for the 1890 Ghost Dance movement, which is dominated by a single classic work, Mooney's.

The tribes, major tribal divisions, or reservations mentioned by Mooney (1896) were narrowed by excluding those who could not reasonably be expected to have heard of the movement. This determination was based primarily on Mooney's comments and his map (pl. LXXXV) showing the approximate area of the 1890 movement and locating tribes and reservations inside or outside the area. Other authors were consulted as well, however: Grinnell (1891), Gilfillan (1901), Kroeber (1925), Spier (1927, 1935), Gayton (1930), Lesser (1933), Hill (1944), Dobyns and Euler (1967), LaBarre (1972), Hittman, (1973), Overholt (1974), Carroll (1975, 1976, 1979), Brown (1976), Heizer (1978), and Landsman (1979). Finally, the Department of Interior's file on the 1890 Ghost Dance (U.S. Bureau of Indian Affairs, n.d.) was also utilized.

Remaining tribal groups were classified as participants or not from these same sources. My primary text was Mooney, either his comments or his map. The other literature mentioned was secondary but proved extremely valuable in instances, such as the discussion of the 1890 Ghost Dance in California by Kroeber (1925), individual authors in Heizer (1978), U.S. Bureau of Indian Affairs (n.d.), and Young, Moristo, and Tenebaum (1976).

I needed to establish appropriate tribal units here also. As for the 1870 movement, subtrial distinctions and geographical designations were generally, though not always, avoided. I followed Mooney when he indicated important subtribal differences, as with the Apache; geographical distinctions, as with the Cheyenne; and/or variations in Ghost Dance participation, as with the Sioux.

Seventy-three tribes were defined as knowing of the 1890 Ghost Dance movement. (See Appendix E.) The same definition of participation was used here as for the 1870 movement: Forty-six tribes were designated participants; twenty-seven tribes were designated nonparticipants. Dates of first performance of this Ghost Dance, or of first knowledge of it, ranged from January 1889 to the winter of 1891–92.

The Sioux of the 1890 Ghost Dance. I imposed the same data requirements in selecting a tribe for the intratribal analysis of the 1890 Ghost Dance movement as for 1870. The tribe that met these requirements was the Sioux, and only the same limited demographic data were available for them as for the Shastan in 1870.

The Sioux were originally of the forests of the upper Midwest, from Lake Superior across the headwaters of the Mississippi River. By the early 1700s they had been driven west by Ojibwe enemies, to the prairies of the Dakotas. They soon adapted to this environment and with the aid of the horse became "the undisputed masters of an immense territory extending . . . from Minnesota to the Rocky Mountains and from the Yellowstone to the Platte" (Mooney, 1896:824).

By 1870 the Sioux had "negotiated" a series of treaties with the U.S. government; as a result they had only reservation lands, although relatively large ones. Soon gold was discovered on Sioux lands in the Black Hills, and thousands of miners and others rushed there. Conflict over the land culminated in the battle with Custer near the Little Big Horn River in southern Montana. A new agreement was established in 1876 whereby the Sioux lost not only their sacred Black Hills but also a large portion of their other previously guaranteed lands. They became dependent on the U.S. government for food, housing, and clothing; the great herds of buffalo basic to their life and culture were slaughtered when their lands were taken.

Even this dismal situation deteriorated, however, as white population pressure increased. In 1889 another "agreement" established several small reservations, at the expense of yet another large portion of land. At this time the Sioux were facing disease, starvation, and death, and they were almost totally dependent on the U.S. government (Mooney 1896:826–27).

Hearing of the dance through contact with other prairie tribes, the Sioux, the Northern Cheyenne, and the Northern Arapaho late in 1889 sent a delegation to talk with Wovoka at Walker Lake, Nevada (Mooney, 1896:894). The delegates of the numerous Sioux bands returned in March 1890, and the Sioux made the decision to "preach" the doctrine of the Ghost Dance (Mooney, 1896:819–21, 843).

They were not the only ones who heard of the Ghost Dance, however. Agents supervising Sioux reservations reported it, often in sensational terms, to their superiors in Washington, D.C. (U.S. Commissioner of Indian Affairs, 1891:124–27), and this was the point at which James Mooney was sent to investigate the movement.

Several thousand troops eventually arrived in Sioux country (Mooney, 1896:850) in readiness for any possible "outbreak." This military occupation seems to have alarmed the Sioux, and thousands fled for refuge to the Bad Lands (Mooney, 1896:851–52). On December 15, 1890, Sitting Bull, a Sioux Ghost Dance leader, was shot to death during his arrest by Indian police; on December 29, 1890, there occurred the massacre at Wounded Knee Creek in which several hundred innocent Sioux were killed.

Perhaps because of these tragic and violent circumstances, the Ghost Dance assumed unique features and uses among the Sioux. The movement among most other Indian peoples lacked overt hostility toward whites and is generally considered to have been peaceful. Among the Sioux, however, because of "chronic dissatisfaction . . . the movement assumed a hostile expression" (Mooney, 1896:777).

As the movement assumed unique uses, so did some practices assume new features. Ghost Dance shirts were used by several Indian peoples in both 1870 and 1890.[3] The Sioux used them extensively, however, and Sioux disciples taught that the wearing of shirts made one immune to the bullets of the troops the Sioux were fighting, as expressed in the following Ghost Dance song (Mooney, 1896:1073):

> Verily, I have given you my strength.
> Says the father, says the father.
> The shirt will cause you to live,
> Says the father, says the father.

---

[3] Mooney (1896:789–91, 916) relates the introduction of the ghost shirts to Mormons. The prophet Wovoka disclaimed any responsibility for them (Mooney, 1896:772).

Using data from the Commissioner of Indian Affairs (1891), Mooney (1896), the U.S. Bureau of the Census (1915), and Utley (1963), I divided the four Sioux divisions used in the tribal analysis into subdivisions and reservation locations. The Santee were divided into Santee per se, Sioux, and Sisseton and Wahpeton; these were then further divided according to their reservation locations. The Teton were divided into the Blackfeet Sioux, Brulé (No. 1 and 2 and Lower), Cuthead, Hunkpapa, Loafer, Minneconjou, Northern, Oglala, Sans Arcs, Two Kettle, and Waziahziah; these were then analyzed by reservation locations. The Yankton Sioux were divided only into reservation areas, the Yanktonnai Sioux into Lower and Upper Yanktonnai and then into reservation locations.

This procedure yielded twenty-seven Sioux subdivisions. Each subdivision was then classified as a participant or not, using data from the Commissioner of Indian Affairs (1891) and Mooney (1896). Sixteen subdivisions were designated as participants, eleven as nonparticipants. (See Appendix F.) Generally, almost all the Teton seem to have participated, and probably most of the Yanktonnai as well; the Santee and Yankton Sioux seem not to have been involved, although they knew of the movement.

Demographic and other data

Obtaining population information on American Indian tribes has historically been problematic for various reasons: lack of full census coverage of American Indians until 1890, tribal movements and relocations, geographical remoteness of American Indian populations, and issues of tribal definition. However, fortuitous circumstances aided me in ascertaining population sizes of interest here.

Populations of the 1870 Ghost Dance. Demographic data on tribes of the 1870 movement are limited for several reasons. First a sudden, massive depopulation of Californian tribes occurred around the mid-1800s. By the 1870 movement, tribes in California were remnants, too small to be of much consequence for census purposes. (See Table 4.3 in Chapter 4.) Second, a reservation system had not been established in California, so tribal populations were not generally located on well-defined geographical areas, which would have made enumerations easier. Third, this Ghost Dance occurred twenty years before the 1890 census of the U.S. population, the first census that even approximated total coverage of American Indians. Fourth, California had a large pre-European Indian population, divided into many tribes and languages, creating a tremendous complexity of tribal definitions.

Despite these problems, there is a tradition of anthropological and historical scholarship on California Indian populations that is of very high quality, and many scholarly accounts of these peoples exist. Publications include, most fortunately, the recently published volume on California of the *Handbook of North American Indians* (Heizer, 1978). Special attention is given in it to the population histories of American Indians, at least partly because of the problems involved in enumerating and estimating these populations. Publications also include, also most fortunately, Kroeber's (1925, 1939, 1957) aboriginal population estimates for California and other areas and Cook's (1976a, 1976c) examinations of the population history of Indians in California. Population sizes for the twentieth century were easier, as published censuses contain these figures.

However, data for all tribal units involved for the periods I wanted – circa 1910, 1890, 1870, 1850, and European contact – were not available from a single source or the same sources. I had to use different sources for each period, including the U.S. Board of Indian Commissioners (1874), U.S. Commissioner of Indian Affairs (1877), U.S. Bureau of the Census (1894), Kroeber (1925), Cook (1976a, 1976c), and Heizer (1978) for the 1890s, 1870s, and 1850s, and Mooney (1928), Baumhoff (1963), Cook and Heizer (1965), and Murdock (1967) for the time of European contact.

My resulting population figures and dates of first European contact are given in Appendixes C and G. Also found in Appendix C are my figures for tribal distance from the origin of the 1870 movement. The primary source of this information is the map of California Indian tribal locations given in Heizer (1978); however, other maps, Mooney's among them, were consulted.

Appendix D gives population figures for the Shastan subgroups analyzed. Figures for the period of the 1870 Ghost Dance were established with data from the U.S. Commissioner of Indian Affairs (1877), the U.S. Bureau of the Census (1915), and Silver (1978). Figures for twenty years earlier were established from Beckham (1971) and Silver (1978). Data for other periods were not available, nor were other data used in the tribal analysis.

No straightforward data for changes in full-bloods were available for tribes of the 1870 Ghost Dance. The only data I found, roughly corresponding to periods of interest, were for the proportion of full-bloods in 1910 (U.S. Bureau of the Census, 1915), forty years after the movement. However, these were available by three age groupings: under twenty, twenty to fifty, and fifty-one years and over. Proportions of full-bloods in each cohort were used as approximations for change over time. Thus the proportion of full-bloods aged fifty-one years or more was used to approximate the proportion at the time of the 1870 Ghost Dance; the proportion of those aged twenty to fifty years to approximate that twenty years after the movement; and the proportion under twenty to approximate that forty years after the movement. Changes were established by subtracting one proportion from the other. These data are present in Appendix G.

Populations of the 1890 Ghost Dance. Circumstances were even more fortuitous for establishing population sizes for tribes of the 1890 Ghost Dance movement.

Mooney gives sizes for many tribes, subtribes, and reservations at about the time of the movement. Also, this Ghost Dance coincided with the 1890 census (U.S. Bureau of the Census, 1894), the first having full coverage of reservation and nonreservation Indian populations; these data supplement Mooney's. Published censuses of 1910 and 1930 contain population figures for these periods. A report of the U.S. Commissioner of Indian Affairs (1877) gives fairly complete population figures for American Indians of the 1870s. And Mooney's (1928) American Indian population estimates for first extensive European contact and his dates of this contact were available.

Unfortunately, data on all tribes for the five periods – circa 1930, 1910, 1890, 1870, and European contact – were not always available from the same source or sources, and I had to utilize various sources for each period, including the U.S. Board of Indian Commissioners (1874, 1875) and Murdock (1967). My resulting population figures and dates of first contact with Europeans are found in Appendixes E and H. Also found in Appendix E are tribal distances from the origin of the 1890 Ghost Dance movement. The source of these is Mooney's (1896) map.

In Appendix F are population figures for Sioux subdivisions. Figures for around 1890 are from U.S. Bureau of the Census (1894, 1915); figures for approximately twenty years earlier are from these censuses as well as from the Board of Indian Commissioners (1874) and Commissioner of Indian Affairs (1877). No further data were available about Sioux subdivisions.

No straightforward data were available for changes in full-bloods for 1890 Ghost Dance tribes. However, data from the 1930 census (U.S. Bureau of the Census, 1937) were available for full-bloods in five-year age groups. These were combined to approximate those used for tribes of the 1870 Ghost Dance. Categories here were nineteen years and under, twenty to forty-nine, and fifty years and over. Differences in proportions of full-bloods in these were used to approximate changes for twenty and forty years after the Ghost Dance. These data are located in Appendix H.

Dichotomizing the variables

Unfortunately, the population data obtained have two potential sources of error. The first is from inherent, historical problems of estimating, enumerating, and reporting figures for American Indian populations. These problems result in error in published figures used either as population sizes or to derive population sizes. The second comes from the impossibility of obtaining population sizes for the same year, from the same source, or on the same tribal unit exactly. This impossibility results in error in comparability of population figures.

Both sources of error are unavoidable and are basically unmeasurable; that is, it is not possible to ascertain the amount of either type of error if, in fact, either is present. It is possible, however, to reduce any error in these data when used for analysis by forming simple dichotomies. Then error results only if a tribe is in the wrong category. Such error may be considered slight, and dichotomies were therefore formed on the population variables. For consistency of analysis, other variables were dichotomized as well.

Dichotomies were formed at points to yield categories of similar size, although it was not always possible to do so when considering noninterval-level data or data with many technical values. Dates of exposure of European contact and the Ghost Dance movements were dichotomized into whole years, as these were the only data typically available, and into similar-sized categories. Distance from origin of the Ghost Dances was also treated in this way, since it was difficult to establish exact tribal boundaries at times of interest. The other interval-level variables of tribal population size, change in size, and percentage of full-blood Indians were dichotomized at the middle of the distributions as far as possible. (This proved especially difficult to do for full-blood percentages: These data contained many identical values.) This step was taken in order not to influence the magnitude, direction, or significance of any resulting relationships. The procedure did, however, produce some lack of comparability between the analysis of the two movements; for example, "large" tribes of the 1870 dance were those of more than 200 members, whereas "large" tribes of the 1890 dance were those of more than 845 members. (See Appendix A.) I do not consider this discrepancy especially problematic, as the groupings of tribes between the movements already represented considerable differences not only in time and geographic area but also in social patterns and cultural content.

The exact points of each dichotomy are shown in Appendix A.

Statistics used

Given these dichotomies, (Kendall's) Q was used to assess magnitude and direction of the relationships and χ^2 (chi-square) to assess their levels of significance.

Q is a simple, nonparametric statistic that may be used on 2×2 tables formed from dichotomous variables. It is defined as

$$Q = \frac{ad - bc}{ad + bc},$$

where a, b, c, and d are cell frequencies. It ranges from -1.0 to $+1.0$. (See Blalock, 1960:231.)

χ^2 is a general test of significance, also appropriate for two dichotomized variables. In 2 × 2 tables, it is expressed as

$$\chi^2 = \frac{N\,(ad-bc)^2}{(a+b)(c+d)(a+c)(b+d)},$$

where a, b, c, and d are cell frequencies and N is number of cases. Level of significance may then be obtained from standard tables indicating probabilities for χ^2 values. (See Blalock, 1960:212–19, 452.)

The use of Q and χ^2 makes my findings comparable to other, recent studies of Ghost Dance participation, as they used the same statistics. (See Carroll, 1975; Brown, 1976; and Landsman, 1979.)

Appendix C. Tribes of the 1870 Ghost Dance: Ghost Dance participation, distance from origin, and population sizes at various times

Tribe	Ghost Dance participation[a]	Date of beginning participation[a]	Miles from origin[b]	Population size — At time of European contact	Date of contact[c]	1850s	1870s
Achumawi	Yes	1871	<300	3,000[d]	1800?	2,000?[e,f]	1,100[e,f,g]
Alseas				2,000?[h,i]	1780	1,000?[f]	
Alsea Subagency	Yes?	1872?	>300	(1,000?)			108[j]
Other	No	1872?	>300	(1,000?)			422[j,k]
Atsugewi	Yes	1871	>300	850[l]	1827	600?[e,f]	450?[d]
Bannock				1,000[i]	1845[h,i]	1,000?[f]	
Ft. Hall	Yes[m]	1870[m]	>300				575[j,m]
Lemhi	Yes?[m]	1870[m]	>300				190[j,m]
Malheur	Yes?[m]	1870[m]	<300				87[m,n]
Cahto	Yes	1874?	<300	1,000[l]	1800?	500[f]	225?[g]
Cahuilla	No[o]	1874?	>300	6,000[l]	1774	3,500[f]	1,181[l]
Calapuya				3,000?[h]	1780[i]	200?[f]	
Grande Ronde	Yes	1871	>300				30[p]
Chilula	Yes?	1871	>300	550[l]	1800?	500[e]	50[f]
Chumash	No	1872?	<300	20,000[q]	1542	1,200?[e]	
Clackamus				2,500[i]	1780[i]	150[f,r]	659[l]
Grande Ronde	No?	1871	>300				100[-,s]
Columbia River	No	1872	>300	2,000[h]	1780[i]		2,000[i]
Coos					1780[i]		
Alsea Subagency	Yes	1872	>300			450?[f]	135[s]
Costanoan	Yes[o]	1871?	<300	11,000[e]	1602	1,000[f]	281[l]
Cupeno	No	1874	>300	625?[f,l]	1795	300?[f]	75[f]

Gabrielino	No	1874?	>300	5,000?	1770	700?f	150?e
Gosiute	Yes?m	1870m	>300		1845i	300?f	256j
Huchnom	Yes?o	1872	<300	2,100l	1850	2,100l	79l
Hupa	No	1872	<300	1,475l	1850	1,475l	641l
Karok	Yes	1871	>300	2,700l	1810?f	1,050?f	1,300l
Klamath				800i	1780i		
Lower End, Klamath Res.	Yes	1870–71	<300				547j,u
Upper End, Klamath Res.	Yes	1870–71	<300				120u
Siletz Res.	Yes	1872	>300				45j
Klickitat	No	1872	>300	1,000?i	1780i	400?d	300?f
Konkow	Yes	1873?	<300	3,000l	1808	2,500?d	159?p
Lassik	Yes?	1874–77	<300	1,411l	1850?	1,411l	175?l
Luiseno	No^o	1874–77	<300	10,000l	1776	2,650f	1,299?f
Maidu	No	1870–71	<300	3,000?l	1825?	2,000?f	1,550e
Mattole	No	1871?	<300	2,476l	1853	2,476l	195?f
Miwok							
Coast	Yes	1872	<300	2,000l	1579	250e	60l
Eastern	Yes	1872	<300	19,500l	1775?	5,000f	1,000?f,j
Lake	Yes	1872	<300	900l	1821	100e	50?f,l
Modoc					1770l		
California	Yes	1871	<300	350?d			159?u
Oregon				350?d			
Lower End, Klamath Res.	Yes?	1870–71	<300				81?u
Upper End, Klamath Res.	Yes	1870–71	<300				130u
Monache	Yes^v	1871^v	<300	1,000?l	1770	800?f	550?l
Navajo	No^w	1872?^w	>300	8,000l	1680i	10,000?x	11,868l
Nisenan	Yes	1872	<300	3,000?l	1790?	900?f	850?l
Nomlaki	Yes	1871	<300	2,000l	1808	1,000?d	190?f,s

Appendix C. (*cont.*)

Tribe	Ghost Dance participation[a]	Date of beginning participation[a]	Miles from origin[b]	Population size — At time of European contact[b,i]	Date of contact[c]	1850s	1870s
Paiute							
California	Yes[v]	1871?[v]	<300	1,500[h,i]	1845[i]	1,500[h]	184[j]
Southern Nevada	Yes[y]	1872?[y]	<300				631[j]
Patwin	Yes	1872	<300	5,000[d]	1800	1,000?[f]	250?[e,f]
Paviotso				3,500?[h]	1845[i]		
California							
Surprise Valley	Yes	1871?	<300				150?[f]
Other	Yes	1871?	<300				175?[f,j]
Nevada							
Pyramid Lake	Yes	1870	<300				500[j]
Walker River	Yes	1870	<300				600[j]
Central	Yes[y]	1870?[y]	<300				195?[f,j]
Oregon							
Silver-Summer, Klamath Res.	Yes	1870–71	<300				128[u]
Warner Valley, Klamath Res.	Yes	1870–71	<300				150[u]
Pomo							
Eastern	Yes	1872	<300	1,260[l]	1776?	800?[e,f]	300?[s]
Northeastern	Yes?	1872?	<300	350[l]	1776?	250?[e,f]	100[s]
Southeastern	Yes	1872	<300	750[l]	1776?	450?[e,f]	100[s]
Western	Yes	1872	<300	9,475[l]	1776?	3,000[e,f]	900?[s]
Santiam				500?[f,i]	1780[i]	250?[f]	
Grande Ronde	Yes	1872	>300				75[p]
Serrano	No[o]	1874?	<300	2,000?[f]	1771	400?[f]	390[s]

Shastan							
Shasta				2,000[g]	1820	1,000?[e,f]	300?[f,s]
California	Yes	1871	<300				72[j]
Grande Ronde, Oregon	Yes	1871	>300				50?[f,s]
Siletz Res., Oregon	Yes	1872	>300	1,000[l]	1820	900?[f]	800?[l]
Other	No	1871	<300	4,500[i]	1845[i]		932[j]
Shoshone							
Idaho						1,000?[f]	
Ft. Hall	Yes[m]	1870[m]	>300				200[p]
Lemhi	Yes?[m]	1870[m]	>300			500?[f]	200?[f]
Wyoming							
Bridger Basin	Yes[m]	1870[m]	>300				200[p]
Other							
Sheepeater	Yes?[m]	1870[m]	<300				86[n]
Snakes	Yes?[m]	1870[m]	<300				300?[m]
Weber	Yes?[m]	1870[m]	>300				300?[l]
Sinkyone							
Lolangkok	No	1874–77	<300	2,145[l]	1853	2,145[l]	275[l]
Shelter Cove	No	1874–77	<300	2,076[l]	1853	2,076[l]	68[p]
Siuslaw				2,000[f,i]	1780[i]	500[l]	
Siletz Res.	Yes	1872	>300	1,600[p]	1780[i]	1,200?[f]	1,070[k]
The Dalles	No	1872	>300	6,000[f,l]	1769	2,250?[f]	886[l]
Tipai-Ipai	No[o]	1874[o]	>300	2,400[i]	1828	316[e]	200[e]
Tolowa	Yes	1872	<300	750?[f]	1776	250[f]	195?[f]
Tubatulabal	No	1874?	<300	550?[i]	1780[i]	700?[f]	
Tututni							
Grande Ronde	Yes	1871	>300				85[p]
Siletz Res.	Yes	1871	>300				189[j]
Umpqua				1,000?[f,i]	1780	250?[f]	
Alsea Subagency	Yes	1872	>300				44[p]
Grande Ronde	Yes	1872	>300				135[p]

68

Appendix C. (cont.)

Tribe	Ghost Dance participation[a]	Date of beginning participation[a]	Miles from origin[b]	Population size At time of European contact	Date of contact[c]	1850s	1870s
Ute				4,500[i,z]	1845[i]		
Capote, Moache and Wiminuchi							
Capote	Yes[m]	1870[m]	>300				147[z]
Moache	Yes[m]	1870[m]	>300				512[z]
Wiminuchi	Yes[m]	1870[m]	>300				250[z]
Pahvant	Yes?[m]	1870[m]	>300				134[k]
Uncompahgre	Yes?[m]	1870[m]	>300				2,290[k]
Unitah							
Reservation	Yes[m]	1870[m]	>300				185?[f,m]
Other	Yes[m]	1870[m]	>300				371?[f,m]
White River							
Parsanveh	Yes[m]	1870[m]	>300				220?[f]
Yampa	Yes[m]	1870[m]	>300				250?[f]
Wailaki	Yes	1874–77	<300	2,760[l]	1853?	2,760[l]	150[e]
Wappo	Yes	1872	<300	4,600	1800?	800[e]	92[f]
Washo				1,000[i]	1845[i]	1,000[i]	
Reno	Yes	1871	<300				100[r]
Other	Yes	1871	<300				450[r,u]
Whilkut	Yes[y]	1871?[y]	<300	500[f]	1850?	500[f]	100?[f,s]
Wintu	Yes?	1872	<300	14,250[l]	1826	6,850[e]	1,000[l]
Wiyot	No	1872?	<300	3,300[l]	1775	900[e]	625[k]
Yana					1821		

North	Yes	1871	<300	500?[f]		350?[d]	100[k]
Yokuts							
Foothill	Yes	1872	<300	9,600[i]	1825?	5,000[e,f]	266?[k]
Northern Valley	Yes	1872	<300	28,252[l]	1769	2,500[e,f]	200?[k]
Southern Valley	Yes	1872	<300	15,700[l]	1772	2,500?[e,f]	254?[k]
Yoncalla							
Grande Ronde	Yes	1871	>300	500?[f,i]	1780[i]		80?[f,s]
Yuki							
Coast	Yes	1874–77	<300	750[e]	1850	750[e]	50[l]
Proper	Yes	1874–77	<300	2,000?[f]	1856	2,000?[f]	238[l]
Yurok	Yes	1872	>300	3,100?[f]	1775	2,450[e]	1,125[e]

[a] Unless indicated otherwise, information in this column was obtained from Du Bois (1939). Other sources, e.g., Spier (1927), Gayton (1930), and Heizer (1978), often provided additional documentation.

[b] Information in this column is from Mooney (1896) and Heizer (1978).

[c] Unless indicated otherwise, information in this column is from the individual tribal chapter in Heizer (1978).

[d] From Cook (1976a).

[e] From Cook (1976c).

[f] Estimated.

[g] From Kroeber (1925).

[h] From Kroeber (1939).

[i] From Mooney (1928).

[j] From U.S. Commissioner of Indian Affairs (1877).

[k] From U.S. Bureau of the Census (1894).

[l] From the individual tribal chapter in Heizer (1978).

[m] From Jorgensen (1972).

[n] From U.S. Commissioner of Indian Affairs (1875).

[o] From Kroeber (1904, 1925).

[p] From U.S. Board of Indian Commissioners (1874).

[q] From Cook and Heizer (1965).

[r] From Du Bois (1939).

[s] From U.S. Bureau of the Census (1915).

[t] From Baumhoff (1963).

[u] From Nash (1955 [1937]).

[v] From Gayton (1930).

[w] From Hill (1944).

[x] From Johnston (1966).

[y] From Spier (1927).

[z] From U.S. Commissioner of Indian Affairs (1873).

Appendix D. *Shastan subdivisions of the 1870 Ghost Dance: population sizes in the 1850s and 1870s*

Shastan subdivisions	Ghost Dance participation[a]	Population size	
		1850s	1870s
Konomihu	No	200?[b,c]	200?[b,c]
New River	No	400[b]	350?[b,c]
Okwanuchu	No	300?[c]	250[b]
Shasta			
California			
Klamath River	Yes	160?[d]	50?[b,c]
Scott Valley	Yes	100?[d]	50?[b,c]
Shasta Valley	Yes	300?[d]	200?[b,c]
Oregon			
Grande Ronde Reservation	Yes	150?[d]	72[e]
Siletz Reservation	Yes	100?[d]	50?[c,f]
Jacksonville	No?[g]	?	50?[c]

[a]Except regarding the Jacksonville Shasta, all information in this column was obtained from Silver (1978).
[b]From Silver (1978).
[c]Estimated.
[d]Derived from information in Beckham (1971).
[e]From U.S. Commissioner of Indian Affairs (1877).
[f]Derived from U.S. Bureau of the Census (1915).
[g]From Du Bois (1939).

Appendix E. Tribes of the 1890 Ghost Dance: Ghost Dance participation, distance from origin, and population sizes at various times

Tribe	Ghost Dance participation[a]	Date[a]	Miles from origin[b]	Population size At time of European contact[c]	Date of contact[c]	1870s[d]	1890s
Arapaho				3,000	1780		
Northern	Yes	1889	<800			1,198	829[e]
Southern	Yes	1889	>800			1,766	1,091[e]
Arikara	Yes	1889?	>800	3,000	1780	670	447[e]
Assiniboin	Yes	1889	>800	10,000	1780	1,719	1,671[e]
Bannock	Yes	1889	<800	1,000	1845	897[f]	589[f]
Caddo	Yes	1889	>800	8,500	1690	643	507[e]
Chemehuevi	Yes	1890	<800	350?[g]	1680	320	350[g]
Cheyenne				3,500	1780		
Northern	Yes	1889	<800			937	1,320[e]
Southern	Yes	1889	>800			2,299	2,119[e]
Cohonino (Hauasupai)	Yes	1890	<800	300	1680	250[h]	172[e]
Comanche	Yes	1890–91?	<800	7,000	1690	1,695	1,598[f]
Crow	No	1890	<800	4,000	1780	3,300	2,287[f]
Delaware	Yes	1889	<800	8,000	1600	114	94[e]
Gosiute	Yes	1889	<800		1845	256?	238?[f]
Gros Ventres	Yes	1889	>800	3,000	1780	600	718[e]
Hidatsa	Yes	1889?	>800	2,500	1780	466	522[f]
Iowa	Yes	1890–91?	>800	1,200	1780	529[i]	267[f]
Jicarilla Apache	No	1890–91?	<800	800	1845	798	808[e]
Kansas	Yes	1890–91?	>800	3,000	1780	500[i]	198[f]

71

Appendix E. (*cont.*)

Tribe	Ghost Dance participation[a]	Date[a]	Miles from origin[b]	Population size — At time of European contact[c]	Date of contact[c]	1870s[d]	1890s
Kichai	Yes	1890	>800	500	1690	90	52[e]
Kickapoo	Yes	1890–91?	>800	2,000	1650	565	514[e]
Kiowa	Yes	1890	>800	2,000	1780	1,090	1,017[e]
Kiowa-Apache	Yes	1890	>800	300	1780	343	224[e]
Mandan	Yes	1889?	>800	3,600	1780	257	400[f]
Mescalero Apache	No	1890–91?	>800	700	1690	550[f]	513[e]
Mohave	No	1890	<800	3,000	1680	1,611	2,100[e]
Navajo	No	1890	<800	8,000	1780	11,868	16,000[e]
Nez Perce	No	1890?	<800	4,000	1780	2,800	1,800[e]
Ojibwe				35,000	1650		
Michigan	No	1890?	>800	10,000?[g]		10,000[j]	4,000[g]
Minnesota							
White Earth	No?[k]	1890?	>800			2,894[j]	2,230[f]
Other	No	1890?	>800	10,000?[g]		3,393?[j]	8,208[f]
Wisconsin	No	1890?	>800	10,000[g]		4,630[j]	4,500?[g]
Omaha	No	1890	>800	2,800	1780	1,061	1,158[f]
Osage	No	1890–91?	>800	6,200	1780	3,000[j]	1,509[f]
Oto-Missouri	Yes	1890–91?	>800	900	1780	452	362[f]
Paiute	Yes	1889	<800	7,500	1780	5,900?[l]	6,815[m]
Paviotso					1780		
California	Yes	1889	<800			184?	110[m]
Nevada							
Duck Valley	Yes	1889	<800			600	209[e]

Pyramid Lake	Yes	1889	<800			500	494^e
Walker River	Yes	1889	<800			600	563^e
Other	Yes	1889	<800			600	152^m
Oregon	Yes	1889	<800			896	341^m
Pawnee	Yes	1891–92	>800	10,000	1780	1,521	804^f
Pit River Indians	Yes	1890	<800		1769	3,000?^{g}	985^m
Ponca	No	1889?	>800	800	1780	753	822^f
Potawatomi	No	1890–91?	>800	4,000	1650	996	942^f
Pueblo Indians							
Acoma	No	1891	<800	1,500	1680	1,650^n	2,190^o
Hopi	No	1891	<800	2,800	1680	1,339	1,970^o
Jemez	No	1891	<800	2,500	1680	450^n	521°
Keres	No	1891	<800	2,500	1680	2,075^n	1,971^o
Taos	Yes	1891	<800	1,500	1680	595^n	509°
Tewa	No	1891	<800	2,500	1680	1,105^n	1,215^o
Tiqua	No	1891	>800	3,000	1680	850^n	1,108^o
Zuni	No	1891	<800	2,500	1680	2,500^n	1,682^o
Sauk and Fox	No	1891	>800	7,500	1650	1,051	1,160^f
Shoshone		1890–91		4,500	1845		
Northern							
Ft. Hall	Yes	1889	<800			932	979^f
Lemhi	Yes	1889	<800			200^i	249^f
Eastern	Yes	1889	<800			1,300?	916^f
Western							
Duck Valley	Yes	1889	<800			368	383^f
Other	Yes	1889	<800			2,000?	1,200?^{f,m}
Sioux							
Santee	No	1889	>800	7,500?^{g}		3,928	3,862^{f,m}
Teton	Yes	1889	>800	20,000^g	1790	18,106	16,556^f
Yankton	No	1890	>800	3,500?^{g}		2,182	1,725^f

Appendix E. (*cont.*)

Tribe	Ghost Dance participation[a]	Date[a]	Miles from origin[b]	Population size			
				At time of European contact[c]	Date of contact[c]	1870s[d]	1890s
Yanktonais	Yes	1890	>800	8,000[g]	?	6,848?	3,965[f]
Tule River Indians	Yes	1889	<800	800?	1845	374	161[f]
Ute				4,500			
Capote, Moache and Wiminuchi	No	1889	<800			909[p]	845[m]
Uncompahgre	Yes	1889	<800			2,290[q]	559?[m]
Unitah and White River	Yes	1889	<800			1,026?[j,r]	1,045?[j,p,r]
Walapai	Yes	1889	<800	700	1680	1,000[q]	350[e]
Washo	Yes	1889	<800	1,000	1845	500[i]	400[e]
Wichita	Yes	1890	>800	3,200	1690	409	316[e]
Winnebago	No	1890	>800	3,800	1650	2,310	1,950[f,m]

[a] All information in this column is from Mooney (1896). Other sources, e.g., Moorehead (1890, 1891), Hill (1944), and Dobyns and Euler (1967), often provided additional documentation. Since the Earth Lodge Cult, the *Bole-Maru*, and the Big Head Cult are considered variations of the Ghost Dance, tribes participating in them were included.

[b] Information in this column is from Mooney (1896) and Heizer (1978).

[c] Unless indicated otherwise, information in this column is from Mooney (1928).

[d] Unless indicated otherwise, information in this column is from U.S. Commissioner of Indian Affairs (1877).

[e] From Mooney (1896).

[f] From U.S. Bureau of the Census (1894).

[g] Estimated.

[h] Estimated from information in Mooney (1896).

[i] From U.S. Board of Indian Commissioners (1874).

[j] From U.S. Commissioner of Indian Affairs (1877).

[k] Information in Gilfillan (1901) and U.S. Bureau of Indian Affairs (n.d.) indicates that the Ojibwe on White Earth Reservation started performing a new dance about the time of the 1890 Ghost Dance movement. It seems unlikely, however, that this was the Ghost Dance per se.

[l] Derived from information in Mooney (1896).

[m] From U.S. Bureau of the Census (1915).

[n] From Schoolcraft (1851–57:vol. 3).

[o] From Mooney (1928).

[p] From U.S. Commissioner of Indian Affairs (1873).

[q] From Murdock (1967).

[r] From Jorgensen (1972).

75

Appendix F. *Sioux subdivisions of the 1890 Ghost Dance: population sizes in the 1870s and 1890s*

Sioux subdivisions	Ghost Dance participation[a]	Population size 1870s	Population size 1890s
Santee			
Santee per se, Nebraska			
Niobrara Reservation	No	744[b]	869[d]
Santee per se, North Dakota			
Devil's Lake Reservation	No		54[d]
Santee per se, South Dakota			
Flandreau Reservation	No	364[b]	292[f]
Sioux, Minnesota	No		100[f]
Sisseton and Wahpeton, North Dakota			
Devil's Lake Reservation, Sisseton	No	900?[c,e]	420[d]
Devil's Lake Reservation, Wahpeton	No		142[d]
Sisseton and Wahpeton, South Dakota			
Lake Traverse Reservation	No	1,715[b]	1,522[d]
Teton			
Blackfeet Sioux, North Dakota			
Standing Rock Reservation	Yes	847?[e]	571[d]
Blackfeet Sioux, South Dakota			
Cheyenne River Reservation	Yes	250?[c,e]	1,000?[c,d]
Brulé, South Dakota			
Rosebud Reservation, Brulé #1	Yes	2,050?[b,c]	1,238[d]
Rosebud Reservation, Brulé #2	Yes	1,400?[b,c]	750[d]
Lower Brulé Reservation, Lower Brulé	Yes	1,200[d]	1,028[d]
Cuthead, North Dakota			
Devil's Lake Reservation	No?	200?[b,c,e]	295[d]
Hunkpapa, North Dakota		2,100[f]	
Standing Rock Reservation	Yes		1,739[d]
Loafer, South Dakota		1,756[b]	
Rosebud Reservation	Yes		1,052[d]
Minneconjou, South Dakota			
Cheyenne River Reservation	Yes	1,800[e]	1,268[f]
Northern Sioux, South Dakota		600?[c]	
Rosebud Reservation	Yes		167[d]
Oglala, South Dakota		10,286[f]	
Pine Ridge Reservation	Yes		6,356[f]
Sans Arcs, South Dakota			
Cheyenne River Reservation	Yes	2,000[e]	950?[c,d]
Two Kettle, South Dakota			
Cheyenne River Reservation	Yes	500?[b,c]	200?[c,d]
Rosebud Reservation	Yes	1,000?[b,c,e]	228[d]

Appendix F. (*cont.*)

Sioux subdivisions	Ghost Dance participation[a]	Population size	
		1870s	1890s
Waziahziah, South Dakota			
Rosebud Reservation	Yes		1,184[d]
Yankton			
North Dakota			
Devil's Lake Reservation	No	400[b,c,e]	123[d]
South Dakota			
Yankton Reservation	No	2,100[b,c,e]	1,725[d]
Yanktonnai			
Lower Yanktonnai, Montana			
Ft. Peck Reservation	Yes?	4,395[b]	1,121[d]
Lower Yanktonnai, South Dakota			
Crow Creek Reservation	No?	1,223[b]	1,058[d]
Upper Yanktonnai, North Dakota		2,900?[d]	
Standing Rock Reservation	Yes		1,786[d]

[a] All information in this column is from Mooney (1896) and U.S. Commissioner of Indian Affairs (1891).
[b] From U.S. Commissioner of Indian Affairs (1877).
[c] Estimated.
[d] From U.S. Bureau of the Census (1894).
[e] From U.S. Board of Indian Commissioners (1874).
[f] From U.S. Board of the Census (1915).

Appendix G. *Tribes of the 1870 Ghost Dance: population sizes in the 1890s and 1910s and percentage full-blood in 1910 by age group*

Tribe	Population size		% full-blood in 1910 by age group[a]		
	1890s[a]	1910s[a]	Under 20	20–50	Over 50
Achumawi	1,500?[b]	985	79.9	87.4	98.4
Alseas		29			
Alsea Subagency			50.0?	70.0?	100.0?
Other			50.0?	70.0?	100.0?
Atsugewi	500[c]	240[c]	87.4	90.8	100.0
Bannock					
Ft. Hall	279?[c,d]	213?	67.8?	81.3?	96.5?

Appendix G. (*cont.*)

Tribe	Population size 1890s[a]	1910s[a]	% full-blood in 1910 by age group[a] Under 20	20–50	Over 50
Lemhi	210?[c,d]	110?	67.8?	81.3?	96.5?
Malheur	100?[c]	100?[c]	67.8?	81.3?	96.5?
Cahto	150?[c]	51	50.0	77.8	100.0
Cahuilla	1,156[e]	755			
Calapuya					
Grande Ronde		5?	0.0	100.00	67.7
Chilula	30[f]		77.8	100.0	100.0
Chumash	300?[e]	38[g]	0.0	7.1	85.7
Clackamus					
Grande Ronde	59[h]	39	45.5	63.6	85.7
Columbia River	1,500?[c]	2,250?[c]	52.5?	66.7?	84.8?
Coos					
Alsea Subagency	73?	93	10.0	40.0	81.8
Costanoan	30[h]	17	?	0.0	50.0
Cupeno	175?[b]	150?[i]	59.3	77.9	84.3
Gabrielino	50?[c]	11	0.0	0.0	100.0
Gosiute	238[d]	270?[c]			
Huchnom	50?[e]	15	0.0	60.0	80.0
Hupa	468[h]	639[e]	39.7	54.5	91.0
Karok	600[h]	775	31.9	50.5	91.3
Klamath	750?[c]	696			
Lower End, Klamath Res.			49.8?	68.2?	97.2?
Upper End, Klamath Res.			49.8?	68.2?	97.2?
Siletz Res.		75[c]	49.8?	68.2?	97.2?
Klickitat	300?[c]	300?[c]	76.5	81.0	95.5
Konkow	300?[c]	450[e]	87.4?	90.8?	100.0?
Lassik	175?[c]	100	22.7?	38.6?	84.1?
Luiseno	1,901[e]	983[e]	64.4	80.3	95.7
Maidu	1,000[b]	1,100[g]	43.7	50.5	92.2
Mattole	50?[c]	34	6.7	37.5	100.0
Miwok					
Coast	50?[c]	22?	31.9?	52.4?	90.3?
Eastern	900?[c]	670?	32.4?	53.5?	91.7?
Lake	20[b]	25[e]	31.9?	52.4?	90.3?
Modoc					
California	200?[c]	26	61.2?	73.0?	100.0?
Oregon	230?[c]	212[e]			
Lower End, Klamath Res.			61.2?	73.0?	100.0?
Upper End, Klamath Res.			61.2?	73.0?	100.0?
Monache	1,000[c]	1,448?[e]	76.0	88.2	98.9

Appendix G. (*cont.*)

Tribe	Population size		% full-blood in 1910 by age group[a]		
	1890s[a]	1910s[a]	Under 20	20–50	Over 50
Navajo	16,000[j]	22,455	99.2	99.5	99.8
Nisenan	750?[c]	450	87.4?	90.8?	100.0?
Nomlaki	160?[c]	125	24.1	34.0	91.7
Paiute					
California	400?[c]	210	83.5?	87.2?	92.9?
Southern Nevada	200	247	83.5?	87.2?	92.9?
Patwin	250?[c]	186	48.7	60.0	80.0
Paviotso					
California	350?[c]	101			
Surprise Valley			84.5?	91.3?	95.0?
Other			84.5?	91.3?	95.0?
Nevada		2,414			
Pyramid Lake	646		84.5?	91.3?	95.0?
Walker River	427		84.5?	91.3?	95.0?
Central	200?[c]		84.5?	91.3?	95.0?
Oregon					
Silver-Summer, Klamath Res.			84.5?	91.3?	95.0?
Warner Valley, Klamath Res.			84.5?	91.3?	95.0?
Pomo	1,450[b]	1,193			
Eastern			58.6	66.7	83.9
Northeastern			41.2	62.2	91.7
Southeastern			83.3	92.2	91.7
Western			73.4	76.7	89.0
Santiam					
Grande Ronde	25[c]	9			
Serrano	200?[c]	118	63.5	78.3	100.0
Shastan					
Shasta					
California	300?[c]	225	14.4?	28.4?	83.7?
Grande Ronde, Oregon	52	128	14.4?	28.4?	83.7?
Siletz Res., Oregon	300?[h]		14.4?	28.4?	83.7?
Other	600?[c]	500?[c]	64.3?	76.0?	95.7?
Shoshone		1,259			
Idaho					
Ft. Hall	980[c]		86.3?	88.7?	98.1?
Lemhi	250[c]		86.3?	88.7?	98.1?
Wyoming					
Bridger Basin	200?[c]		86.3?	88.7?	98.1?
Other					
Sheepeater			86.3?	88.7?	98.1?

Appendix G. (*cont.*)

Tribe	Population size 1890s[a]	Population size 1910s[a]	% full-blood in 1910 by age group[a] Under 20	% full-blood in 1910 by age group[a] 20–50	% full-blood in 1910 by age group[a] Over 50
Snakes			86.3?	88.7?	98.1?
Weber			86.3?	88.7?	98.1?
Sinkyone					
Lolangkok	150?[c]	100[e]	22.7?	38.6?	84.1?
Shelter Cove	150?[c]	100[e]	22.7?	38.6?	84.1?
Siuslaw					
Siletz Res.	25?[c]	7?	0.0	75.0	67.0
The Dalles	150?[c]	50?[c]	52.5?	66.7?	84.8?
Tipai-Ipai	600?[c,e]	500?[c,e]	67.1?	84.3?	94.7?
Tolowa	200?[c]	121	47.3	70.8	100.0
Tubatulabal	150?[c]	105	68.0	73.2	100.0
Tututni	450?[c]	383[e]			
Grande Ronde			42.3?	57.5?	96.3?
Siletz Res.			42.3?	57.5?	96.3?
Umpqua					
Alsea Subagency	75?[c]	100?	39.6?	60.0?	81.0?
Grande Ronde	80[h]	9	39.6?	60.0?	81.0?
Ute					
Capote, Moache and Wiminuchi	845[d]				
Capote		64	91.9?	95.7?	99.1?
Moache		156	91.9?	95.7?	99.1?
Wiminuchi		241	91.9?	95.7?	99.1?
Pahvant	?	37	91.9?	95.7?	99.1?
Uncompahgre	559?[d]	412	91.9?	95.7?	99.1?
Unitah		373			
Reservation	200?[c,k]		91.9?	95.7?	99.1?
Other	375[c,k]		91.9?	95.7?	99.1?
White River					
Parsanveh	220?[c]	300?[c]	91.9?	95.7?	99.1?
Yanpa	250?[c,l]	320?[c]	91.9?	95.7?	99.1?
Wailaki	200?[b]	225[e]	10.0	40.8	97.6
Wappo	50[b]	73	47.9	69.4	100.0
Washo		819			
Reno	200[d]		66.2?	83.2?	99.1?
Other	500?[c]		66.2?	83.2?	99.1?
Whilkut	100?[c]	76	45.5	80.8	100.0
Wintu	800?[c]	399	11.0	29.3	83.6
Wiyot	200?[c]	152	25.7	45.8	91.2
Yana	35[h]	39			

Appendix G. (*cont.*)

Tribe	Population size 1890s[a]	1910s[a]	% full-blood in 1910 by age group[a] Under 20	20–50	Over 50
Central North Yokuts	600[b]				
Foothill		302[g]	82.8	83.8	90.9
Northern Valley		187[g]	50.5?	59.3?	85.0?
Southern Valley		150?[c]	50.5?	59.3?	85.0?
Yoncalla Grande Ronde	50?[c]	11	0.0	75.0	100.0
Yuki Coast	45?[c]	15	52.1?	69.1?	97.8?
Proper	168?[e]	95	52.1?	69.1?	97.8?
Yurok	900[b]	668	66.7	45.1	98.3

[a]Unless indicated otherwise, information in these columns is from U.S. Bureau of the Census (1915).
[b]From Cook (1976c).
[c]Estimated.
[d]From U.S. Commissioner of Indian Affairs (1877).
[e]From the individual tribal chapter in Heizer (1978).
[f]From Cook (1976a).
[g]From Kroeber (1957).
[h]From Powell (1891).
[i]From Kroeber (1925).
[j]From Johnston (1966).
[k]From Jorgensen (1972).
[l]From U.S. Commissioner of Indian Affairs (1873).

Appendix H. *Tribes of the 1890 Ghost Dance: population sizes in the 1910s and 1930s and percentage full-blood in 1930 by age group*

Tribe	Population size 1910s[a]	1930s[b]	% full-blood in 1930 by age group[c] Under 20	20–49	Over 40
Arapaho Northern	721	867	70.1?	75.0?	90.1?
Southern	685	360?	70.1?	75.0?	90.1?
Arikara	44	420	51.6	60.9	76.3

Appendix H. (*cont.*)

Tribe	Population size 1910s[a]	1930s[b]	% full-blood in 1930 by age group[c] Under 20	20–49	Over 40
Assiniboin	1,253	1,581	26.4	31.2	78.8
Bannock	413	415	35.6	44.1	76.9
Caddo	452	625	52.7	58.3	78.9
Chemehuevi	355	375?[d]	64.9?	69.9?	85.7?
Cheyenne					
Northern	1,346	1,408	74.1?	77.5?	91.3?
Southern	1,522	1,220	74.1?	77.5?	91.3?
Cohonino (Havasupai)	174	197	92.2?	92.8?	95.0?
Comanche	1,171	1,423	34.7	39.0	60.9
Crow	1,799	1,674	51.4	56.0	87.1
Delaware	914?	971?	9.6	17.0	42.6
Gosiute	270?	250?			
Gros Ventres (Atsina)	510	631	30.2	35.6	85.1
Hidatsa (Minitari)	547	644?	49.5	56.0	78.5
Iowa	244	176	25.0	27.2	61.1
Jicarilla Apache	694	600?[d]	67.7	68.1	68.7
Kansas	238	318	12.4	19.7	67.9
Kichai	10	15?	83.8	88.5	92.1
Kickapoo	348	523	43.4	47.1	54.0
Kiowa	1,126	1,050	50.9	53.1	62.9
Kiowa-Apache	139	184	28.7	37.5	75.0
Mandan	209	271	55.2	59.8	92.9
Mescalero Apache	424	400?[d]	67.7	68.1	68.7
Mission Indians					
Mohave	1,058	854	93.2	94.7	99.4
Navajo	22,455	39,064	97.2	97.2	97.7
Nez Perce	1,259	1,090?	59.2?	62.4?	79.5?
Ojibwe					
Michigan	3,725	1,685	13.6?	16.1?	35.2?
Minnesota	8,234	9,495			
White Earth			13.6?	16.1?	35.2?
Other			13.6?	16.1?	35.2?
Wisconsin	4,299	4,437	13.6?	16.1?	35.2?
Omaha	1,105	1,103	78.7	81.3	87.2
Osage	1,373	2,344?	18.7	21.4	38.4
Oto-Missouri	390	627	50.4	53.1	72.2
Paiute	6,500?[d]	7,000[d]	64.9?	69.9?	85.7?
Paviotso					
California	150?[d]	382?	39.1?	43.7?	71.1?
Nevada	2,414	2,660			

Appendix H. (*cont.*)

Tribe	Population size		% full-blood in 1930 by age group[c]		
	1910s[a]	1930s[b]	Under 20	20–49	Over 40
Duck Valley			39.1?	43.7?	71.1?
Pyramid Lake	646?		39.1?	43.7?	71.1?
Walker River			39.1?	43.7?	71.1?
Other			39.1?	43.7?	71.1?
Oregon	350?[d]	375?[d]	39.1?	43.7?	71.1?
Pawnee	633	770	60.8	67.5	88.1
Pit River Indians	710	508	52.9?	66.4?	84.4?
Ponca	619	313?	16.5	22.3	46.9
Potawatomi	866?	636?	33.0?	35.9?	49.3?
Pueblo					
Acoma	2,163	2,100?[d]	97.0?	97.5?	99.6?
Hopi	1,941	2,701?	96.8?	96.8?	99.2?
Jemez	499	634[e]	92.4?	94.3?	98.0?
Keres	1,864	2,191[e]	97.0?	97.5?	98.7?
Taos	517	791[e]	92.4?	94.3?	98.0?
Tewa	881?	1,200?[e]	92.4?	94.3?	98.0?
Tigua	800?[d]	915?[e]	92.4?	94.3?	98.0?
Zuni	1,667	1,749			
Sauk and Fox	724	887	74.9	68.9	79.2
Shoshone					
Northern	1,259	1,251			
Ft. Hall			49.5?	58.6?	84.2?
Lemhi			49.5?	58.6?	84.2?
Eastern	700	787	49.5?	58.6?	84.2?
Western	1,600	1,633			
Duck Valley			49.5?	58.6?	84.2?
Other			49.5?	58.6?	84.2?
Sioux					
Santee	5,048		43.7?	48.7?	75.8?
Teton	14,284		43.7?	48.7?	75.8?
Yankton	2,088		43.7?	48.7?	75.8?
Yanktonais	1,375?		43.7?	48.7?	75.8?
Tule River Indians	200?[d]	175?[d]			
Ute		1,269			
Capote, Moache and					
Wiminuchi	461		79.8?	83.2?	93.3?
Uncompahgre	412?		79.8?	83.2?	93.3?
Unitah and White					
River	893		79.8?	83.2?	93.3?
Walapai	501	449	92.2?	92.8?	95.0?

Appendix H. (*cont.*)

| Tribe | Population size | | % full-blood in 1930 by age group[c] | | |
	1910s[a]	1930s[b]	Under 20	20–49	Over 40
Washo	819	668	70.0	74.3	96.2
Wichita	318	328	83.8?	88.5?	92.1?
Winnebago	1,820	1,446	74.8	75.0	76.4

[a]Unless indicated otherwise, figures in this column are from U.S. Bureau of the Census (1915); Mooney (1928) was also consulted.
[b]Unless indicated otherwise, figures in this column are from U.S. Bureau of the Census (1937).
[c]All information in this column is from U.S. Bureau of the Census (1937).
[d]Estimated.
[e]From Ortiz (1979).

References

Aberle, David F.
1959   "The Prophet Dance and Reactions to White Contact." *Southwestern Journal of Anthropology* 15:74–83.

Ashburn, Percy
1947   *The Ranks of Death: A Medical History of the Conquest of America.* New York: Coward-McCann.

Bailey, Paul
1957   *Wovoka, the Indian Messiah.* Los Angeles: Westernlore Press.

Barber, Bernard
1941   "Acculturation and Messianic Movements." *American Sociological Review* 6:663–69.

Baumhoff, Martin A.
1963   "Ecological Determinants of Aboriginal California Populations." *University of California Publications in American Archaeology and Ethnology* 49:155–236.

Bean, Lowell John, and Sylvia Brakke Vane
1978   "Cults and Their Transformations." Pp. 662–72 in Robert Heizer, ed., *Handbook of North American Indians,* Vol. 8: *California.* Washington, DC: U.S. Government Printing Office.

Beckham, Stephen Dow
1971   *Requiem for a People: The Rogue Indians and the Frontiersmen.* Norman: University of Oklahoma Press.

Blalock, Hubert M.
1960   *Social Statistics.* New York: McGraw-Hill.

Bourke, John G.
1890   "The Indian Messiah." *Nation* 1327:439–40.

Brown, Kaye
1976   "Quantitative Testing and Revitalization Behavior: On Carroll's Explanation of the Ghost Dance." *American Sociological Review* 40:389–401.

Carroll, Michael
1975   "Revitalization Movements and Social Structure: Some Quantitative Tests." *American Sociological Review* 41:389–401.
1976   "Reply to Brown." *American Sociological Review* 41:744–46.
1979   "Rejoinder to Landsman." *American Sociological Review* 44:166–68.

Champagne, Duane
1983   "Social Structure, Revitalization Movements and State Building: Social Change in Four Native American Societies." *American Sociological Review* 48:754–63.
1985   "Cherokee Social Movements: A Response to Thornton." *American Sociological Review* 50:127–30.

85

Cohn, Norman
1970   *The Pursuit of the Millennium*. New York: Oxford University Press.
Cook, Sherburne Friend
1943   "Migration and Urbanization of the Indians in California." *Human Biology* 15:33–45.
1973   "Interracial Warfare and Population Decline among the New England Indians." *Ethnohistory* 20:1–24.
1976a   *The Population of the California Indians, 1769–1970*. Berkeley: University of California Press.
1976b   *The Indian Population of New England in the Seventeenth Century*. Berkeley: University of California Press.
1976c   *The Conflict between the California Indians and White Civilization*. Berkeley: University of California Press.
Cook, Sherburne Friend, and Robert F. Heizer
1965   "The Quantitative Approach to the Relation between Population and Settlement Size." *University of California Archaeology Survey Reports* 64:1–97.
Crosby, Alfred W., Jr.
1972   *The Columbian Exchange: Biological and Cultural Consequences of 1492*. Westport, CT: Greenwood.
DeMallie, Raymond J.
1982   "The Lakota Ghost Dance: An Ethnohistorical Account." *Pacific Historical Review* 51:385–405.
Denevan, William M.
1976   "Introduction." Pp. 1–12 in William M. Denevan, ed., *The Native Population of the Americas in 1492*. Madison: University of Wisconsin Press.
Dobyns, Henry F.
1966   "Estimating Aboriginal American Population: An Appraisal of Techniques with a New Hemispheric Estimate." *Current Anthropology* 7:395–416.
1976   *Native American Historical Demography: A Critical Bibliography*. Bloomington: Indiana University Press.
1983   *Their Number Become Thinned: Native American Population Dynamics in Eastern North America*. Knoxville: University of Tennessee Press.
Dobyns, Henry F., and R. C. Euler
1967   *The Ghost Dance of 1889 among the Pai Indians of Northwestern Arizona*. Prescott, AZ: Prescott College Press.
Driver, Harold E.
1968   "On the Population Nadir of Indians in the United States." *Current Anthropology* 9:30.
1974   *Comparative Studies by Harold E. Driver and Essays in His Honor*. Edited by Joseph G. Jorgensen. New Haven: HRAF Press.
Du Bois, Cora
1939   *The 1870 Ghost Dance*. Anthropological Records 3. Berkeley: University of California Press.
Eastman, Elaine Goodale
1945   "The Ghost Dance War and Wounded Knee Massacre of 1890–91." *Nebraska History* 26:26–42.
Erikson, Kai
1966   *Wayward Puritans: A Study in the Sociology of Deviance*. New York: Wiley.
Ewers, John C.
1973   "The Influence of Epidemics on the Indian Population and Cultures of Texas." *Plains Anthropologist* 18:104–15.

Fletcher, Alice C.
1891   "The Indian Messiah." *Journal of American Folk-Lore* 4:57–60.

Ford, J. A., and Gordon R. Wiley
1941   "An Interpretation of the Prehistory of the Eastern United States." *American Anthropologist*, n.s., 43:325–63.

Fried, Morton
1975   *The Notion of Tribe*. Menlo Park, CA: Cummings.

Gayton, A. H.
1930   "The Ghost Dance of 1870 in South-central California." *University of California Publications in American Archaeology and Ethnology* 28:57–82.

Gilfillan, Joseph
1901   "The Ojibways in Minnesota." *Minnesota Historical Society Collections* 9:55–128.

Grinnell, George Bird
1891   "Account of the Northern Cheyennes concerning the Messiah Superstition." *Journal of American Folk-Lore* 4:61–68.

Hadley, J. Nixon
1957   "The Demography of American Indians." *Annals of the American Academy of Political and Social Science* 311:23–30.

Hall, Thomas D.
1983   "Peripheries, Regions of Refuge, and Nonstate Societies: Toward a Theory of Reactive Social Change." *Social Quarterly* 64:582–97.

Heizer, Robert F., ed.
1978   *Handbook of North American Indians*, Vol. 8: *California*. Washington, DC: U.S. Government Printing Office.

Herzog, George
1935   "Plains Ghost Dance and Great Basin Music." *American Anthropologist*, n.s., 37:403–19.

Hill, W. W.
1944   "The Navaho Indians and the Ghost Dance of 1890." *American Anthropologist*, n.s., 46:523–27.

Hittman, Michael
1973   "The 1870 Ghost Dance at the Walker River Reservation: A Reconstruction." *Ethnohistory* 20:247–78.

Hornaday, William T.
1889   *The Extermination of the American Bison*. Washington, DC: U.S. Government Printing Office.

Institute for the Development of Indian Law
n.d.a   *Treaties and Agreements of the Indian Tribes of the Northern Plains*. The American Indian Treaties Series. Washington, DC: Institute for the Development of Indian Law.

n.d.b   *Treaties and Agreements of the Indian Tribes of the Pacific Northwest*. The American Indian Treaties Series. Washington, DC: Institute for the Development of Indian Law.

Jenkins, J. Craig
1983   "Resource Mobilization Theory and the Study of Social Movements." *Annual Review of Sociology* 9:527–53.

Johnston, Denis Foster
1966   *An Analysis of Sources of Information on the Population of the Navaho*. Smithsonian Institution, Bureau of American Ethnology, Bulletin 197. Washington, DC: U.S. Government Printing Office.

Jorgensen, Joseph G.
1972   *The Sun Dance Religion*. Chicago: University of Chicago Press.
Kehoe, Alice B.
1968   "The Ghost Dance Religion in Saskatchewan, Canada." *Plains Anthropologist* 13:296–304.
Killian, Lewis M.
1984   "Organization, Rationality and Spontaneity in the Civil Rights Movement." *American Sociological Review* 49:770–83.
Klandermans, Bert
1984   "Social-Psychological Explanations of Resource Mobilization Theory." *American Sociological Review* 49:583–600.
Kroeber, Alfred L.
1904   "A Ghost-dance in California." *Journal of American Folk-Lore* 17:32–35.
1925   *Handbook of the Indians of California*. Washington, DC: U.S. Government Printing Office.
1939   "Cultural and Natural Areas of Native North America." *University of California Publications in American Archaeology and Ethnology* 38:1–242.
1957   "The California Indian Population about 1910." *University of California Publications in American Archaeology and Ethnology* 47:218–25.
La Barre, Weston
1970   *The Ghost Dance: Origins of Religion*. Garden City, NY: Doubleday.
Landsman, Gail
1979   "The Ghost Dance and the Policy of Land Allotment." *American Sociological Review* 44:162–66.
Lanternari, Vittoria
1963   *The Religions of the Oppressed*. New York: Knopf.
Lesser, Alexander
1933   "Cultural Significance of the Ghost Dance." *American Anthropologist*, n.s., 35:108–15.
Linton, Ralph
1943   "Nativistic Movements." *American Anthropologist*, n.s., 45:231–40.
McHugh, Tom
1972   *The Time of the Buffalo*. New York: Knopf.
Mallery, Garrick
1877   "The Former and Present Number of Our Indians." *American Association for the Advancement of Science, Proceedings* 26:340–66.
Maus, Marion P.
1890   "The New Indian Messiah." *Harper's Weekly* 34:947.
Meader, Forrest W., Jr.
1967   "Na'ilde': The Ghost Dance of the White Mountain Apache." *Kiva* 33:15–24.
Merriam, C. Hart
1905   "The Indian Population of California." *American Anthropologist*, n.s., 7:594–606.
Mooney, James
1896   *The Ghost-Dance Religion and the Sioux Outbreak of 1890*. Pp. 641–1136 in *Fourteenth Annual Report of the United States Bureau of Ethnology to the Secretary of the Smithsonian Institution, 1892–93*, Part 2. Washington, DC: U.S. Government Printing Office.
1910a "Population." Pp. 286–87 in Frederich Webb Hodge, ed. *Handbook of American Indians North of Mexico*. Washington, DC: U.S. Government Printing Office.
1910b "The Indian Ghost Dance." *Collections of the Nebraska State Historical Society*, 16:168–86.

1928 *The Aboriginal Population of America North of Mexico.* Smithsonian Institution, Miscellaneous Collection 80. Washington, DC: U.S. Government Printing Office.

Moorehead, Warren K.
1890 "The Indian Messiah and the Ghost Dance." *American Antiquarian* 13:161–67.
1891 "Ghost Dances in the West." *Illustrated American* 5:327–33.

Morse, Jedediah
1970 *A Report to the Secretary of War of the United States on Indian Affairs.* New York: Au-
(1822) gustus M. Kelley.

Murdock, George
1967 *Ethnographic Atlas.* Pittsburgh: University of Pittsburgh Press.

Nash, Philleo
1955 "The Place of Religious Revivalism in the Formation of the Intercultural Community
(1937) on Klamath Reservation." Pp. 377–442 in Fred Eggan, ed., *Social Anthropoloy of
the North American Tribes.* Chicago: University of Chicago Press.

Olzak, Susan
1983 "Contemporary Ethnic Mobilization." *Annual Review of Sociology* 9:355–74.

Ortiz, Alfonso, ed.
1979 *Handbook of North American Indians,* Vol. 9: *Southwest.* Washington, DC: U.S. Government Printing Office.

Overholt, Thomas W.
1974 "The Ghost Dance of 1890 and the Nature of the Prophetic Process." *Ethnohistory* 21:37–63.

Palmer, Edward Nelson
1948 "Cultural Contacts and Population Growth." *American Journal of Sociology* 53:258–62.

Paredes, J. Anthony, and Kenneth J. Plante
1982 "A Reexamination of Creek Indian Population Trends: 1738–1832." *American Indian
Culture and Research Journal* 6:3–28.

Phister, First Leit. Nat. P.
1891 "The Indian Messiah." *American Anthropologist* 4:105–08.

Powell, John Wesley
1891 "Indian Linguistic Families of America North of Mexico." Pp. 7–142 in *Seventh Annual
Report of the United States Bureau of Ethnology for the Year 1885–1886.* Washington, DC: U.S. Government Printing Office.

Powers, Stephen
1877 *Tribes of California. Contributions to North American Ethnology.* Vol. 3. Washington,
DC: U.S. Government Printing Office.

Remington, Frederic
1890 "The Art of War and Newspaper Men." *Harper's Weekly* 34:947.
1891 "The Sioux Outbreak in South Dakota." *Harper's Weekly* 35:61, 62, 64–65.

Roe, Frank
1970 *The North American Buffalo: A Critical Study of the Species in Its Wild State.* 2d ed.
Toronto: University of Toronto Press.

Schoolcraft, Henry R.
1851–57 *History and Statistical Information respecting the History, Condition and Prospects of
the Indian Tribes of the United States.* 6 vols. Philadelphia: Lippincott, Grambo
& Co.

Seton, Ernest Thompson
1909 *Life-Histories of Northern Animals,* Vol. 1. New York: Scribner.
1929 *Lives of Game Animals,* Vol. 3, Part 2. Garden City, NY: Doubleday, Doran.

Silver, Shirley
  1978   "Shastan Peoples." Pp. 211–24 in Robert Heizer, ed. *Handbook of North American Indians*, Vol. 8: *California*. Washington, DC: U.S. Government Printing Office.
Smith, Maurice G.
  1928   "Notes on the Depopulation of Aboriginal America." *American Anthropologist*, n.s., 30:669–74.
Spier, Leslie
  1927   "The Ghost Dance of 1870 among the Klamath of Oregon." *University of Washington Publications in Anthropology* 2:39–56.
  1935   *The Prophet Dance of the Northwest and Its Derivatives: The Source of the Ghost Dance.* General Series in Anthropology. Menasha, WI: George Banta.
Stewart, Omer C.
  1977   "Contemporary Document on Wovoka (Jack Wilson), Prophet of the Ghost Dance in 1890." *Ethnohistory* 24:219–22.
Strong, William Duncan
  1945   "The Occurrence and Wider Implications of a 'Ghost Cult' on the Columbia River Suggested by Carvings in Wood, Bone and Stone." *American Anthropologist*, n.s., 47:244–61.
Swagerty, William R., and Russell Thornton
  1982   "Preliminary 1980 Census Counts for American Indians, Eskimos and Aleuts: A Research Note." *American Indian Culture and Research Journal* 16:92–93.
Suttles, Wayne
  1957   "The Plateau Prophet Dance among the Coast Salish." *Southwestern Journal of Anthropology* 13:352–96.
Thomas, Robert K.
  1961   "The Redbird Smith Movement." *United States Bureau of American Ethnology Bulletin 180,* 161–66.
Thornton, Russell
  1978   "Implications of Catlin's American Indian Population Estimates for Revision of Mooney's Estimate." *American Journal of Physical Anthropology* 49:11–14.
  1980   "Recent Estimates of the Prehistoric California Indian Population." *Current Anthropology* 21:702–04.
  1981   "Demographic Antecedents of a Revitalization Movement: Population Change, Population Size and the 1890 Ghost Dance." *American Sociological Review* 46:88–96.
  1982   "Demographic Antecedents of Tribal Participation in the 1870 Ghost Dance Movement." *American Indian Culture and Research Journal* 6:79–91.
  1984a   "Cherokee Population Losses during the 'Trail of Tears' Period: A New Perspective and A New Estimate." *Ethnohistory* 31:289–300.
  1984b   "Social Organization and Demographic Survival of the Tolowa." *Ethnohistory* 31:187–96.
  1984c   "Nineteenth-Century Cherokee Revitalization Movements." Paper presented at the 1984 Meeting of the American Society for Ethnohistory, New Orleans.
  1985   "Nineteenth-Century Cherokee History (A Comment)." *American Sociological Review* 50:124–27.
  in press a   *As Snow before a Summer Sun: The Demographic Destruction and Survival of North American Indians* [tentative title]. Norman: University of Oklahoma Press.
  in press b   "History, Structure and Survival: A Comparison of the Yuki (Unkomno'n) and Tolowa (Hush) Indians of Northern California." *Ethnology*.
Thornton, Russell, and Joan Marsh-Thornton

1981 "Estimating Prehistoric American Indian Population Size for United States Area: Implications of the Nineteenth Century Population Decline and Nadir." *American Journal of Physical Anthropology* 55:47–53.

Thurman, Melburn D.
1984 "The Shawnee Prophet's Movement and the Origins of the Prophet Dance." *Current Anthropology* 25:530–31.

Tilly, Charles
1978 *From Mobilization to Revolution.* Reading, MA: Addison-Wesley.

Traugott, Mark
1978 "Reconsidering Social Movements." *Social Problems* 26:38–49.

Ubelaker, Douglas H.
1976 "Prehistoric New World Population Size: Historical Review and Current Appraisal of North American Estimates." *American Journal of Physical Anthropology* 45:661–66.

U.S. Board of Indian Commissioners
1874 *Fifth Annual Report of the Board of Indian Commissioners to the President of the United States, 1873.* Washington, DC: U.S. Government Printing Office.

1875 *Sixth Annual Report of the Board of Indian Commissioners to the President of the United States, 1874.* Washington, DC: U.S. Government Printing Office.

U.S. Bureau of Indian Affairs
1943 "In Fifty Years There May Be As Many Indians As Before the White's Man's Arrival." *Indians at Work* 11:25–28.

U.S. Bureau of Indian Affairs (National Archives)
n.d. Special Case 188, RG 75, Containing Indian Bureau Correspondence Relating Specifically to the Ghost Dance Troubles.

U.S. Bureau of the Census
1894 *Report on Indians Taxed and Indians Not Taxed in the United States, 1890.* Washington, DC: U.S. Government Printing Office.

1915 *Indian Population of the United States and Alaska: 1910.* Washington, DC: U.S. Government Printing Office.

1937 *The Indian Population of the United States and Alaska: 1930.* Washington, DC: U.S. Government Printing Office.

1983 *Ancestry of the Population by State: 1980.* 1980 Census of Population, Supplementary Report PC80–51–10. Washington, DC: U.S. Government Printing Office.

U.S. Commissioner of Indian Affairs
1873 *Annual Report of the Commissioner of Indian Affairs to the Secretary of the Interior for the Year 1873.* Washington, DC: U.S. Government Printing Office.

1875 *Annual Report of the Commissioner of Indian Affairs to the Secretary of the Interior for the Year 1875.* Washington, DC: U.S. Government Printing Office.

1877 *Annual Report of the Commissioner of Indian Affairs to the Secretary of the Interior for the Year 1877.* Washington, DC: U.S. Government Printing Office.

1891 *Annual Report of the Commissioner of Indian Affairs to the Secretary of the Interior for the Year 1891.* Washington, DC: U.S. Government Printing Office.

Unrau, William E.
1973 "The Depopulation of the Dheghia-Siouan Kansa Prior to Removal." *New Mexico Historical Review* 48:313–28.

Utley, Robert M.
1963 *The Last Days of the Sioux Nation.* New Haven: Yale University Press.

Walker, Deward E.
1969 "New Light on the Prophet Dance Controversy." *Ethnohistory* 13:245–55.

Walker, Ernest P.
1983   *Walker's Mammals of the World.* 4th ed. Vol. 2 Baltimore: Johns Hopkins University
(1964)   Press.
Wallace, Anthony
1956   "Revitalization Movements." *American Anthropologist,* n.s., 58:264–81.
Wolf, Eric R.
1982   *Europe and the People without History.* Berkeley: University of California Press.
Worsley, Peter
1957   *The Trumpet Shall Sound.* London: MacGibbon & Kee.
Young, James R., Dennis Moristo, and G. David Tenebaum
1976   *An Inventory of the Mission Indian Agency Records.* American Indian Treaties Publication Series, No. 3. American Indian Studies Center, University of California, Los
Angeles.

Index

Aberle, David F., 12, 13, 15n
American Indian depopulation and Ghost
Dances, 17–18, 20–27; *see also* American
Indian population size
American Indian population size, 20–23; in
California, 24–25, 59–60; decline in, 25–26;
nadir of, 21n, 23, 24–25, 39, 46; in North
America, 21–23; recovery of, 24; in Western
Hemisphere, 20; *see also* American Indian
depopulation and Ghost Dances
area covered by Ghost Dances, 1; 1870, 4–5;
1890, 9; *map,* 2; *see also* diffusion of Ghost
Dances; Ghost Dances in California; Ghost
Dances in Nevada; Ghost Dances in Oregon;
Navajo and 1890 Ghost Dance; Pawnee and
1890 Ghost Dance; Shastan peoples and 1870
Ghost Dance; Sioux and 1890 Ghost Dance;
tribes of Ghost Dances
Ashburn, Percy, 25

Bailey, Paul, 12
Barber, Bernard, 13, 14, 17, 18, 49
battle of Little Big Horn, 57; *see also* Sioux
and 1890 Ghost Dance
Baumhoff, Martin A., 60, 69n
Bean, Lowell John, 5, 6, 13, 48
Beckham, Stephen Dow, 56, 60, 70n
Big Head Cult, 5, 6, 38
Black Hills, 57; *see also* Sioux and 1890 Ghost
Dance
Blalock, Hubert M., 62, 63
Bole-Maru, 5, 6, 12, 38
Bosque Redondo, 14; *see also* Navajo and 1890
Ghost Dance
Bourke, John G., 12
Brown, Kaye, 15, 17, 56, 63
buffalo, 15, 18, 50, 57; American Indian tribes
dependent on, 26; *Bison bison athabascae,*
26; *Bison bison bison,* 26; population history
of, 26–27
Bureau of American Ethnology, 11

Carroll, Michael, 14, 15, 16, 56, 63
Champagne, Duane, xii, 15, 49
Cohn, Norman, 18
Cook, Sherburne Friend, 25, 25n, 43, 60, 69n,
81n
Crosby, Alfred W., Jr., 25
Crow Dance, 8
"Cutter, The," *see* Wovoka

Delaware Prophet, 12; *see also* revitalization
movements; social movements
DeMallie, Raymond J., 13, 48
demographic revitalization, xi, 28, 46–47; hypothesis of, 17–19; test of hypothesis of,
20–27, 29–33, 33–34; variables used to test
hypothesis of, 28–29
Denevan, William M., 20
dichotomizing variables of analysis, 61–62
diffusion of Ghost Dances, 34–36; *see also*
area covered by Ghost Dances; tribes of
Ghost Dances
Dobyns, Henry F., 7, 8, 12, 13, 14, 17, 20,
21, 21n, 24n, 50, 56, 74n
Driver, Harold E., 21n, 35
Du Bois, Cora, 1n, 2, 3, 3n, 4, 5, 6, 11, 12,
13, 14, 39, 54, 55, 56, 69n, 70n
duration of Ghost Dances: 1870, 6; 1890, 10

Earth Lodge Cult, 5, 12, 38
Eastman, Elaine Goodale, 12
Erikson, Kai, 49
Euler, R. C., 7, 8, 12, 13, 14, 17, 56, 74n
Ewers, John C., 25

Fletcher, Alice C., 7, 12, 13
Ford, J. A., 18
Fried, Morton, 54n

Gayton, A. H., 4, 6, 11, 47, 48, 54, 56, 69n
Ghost Dance facial painting: 1870, 3, 4
Ghost Dance names: 1890, 7

93